Chaos Magic for Skeptics

Carlos Atanes

Copyright © 2022 Carlos Atanes
First edition

All rights reserved. No part of this work may be reproduced or utilized in any form by any means electronic or mechanical, including *xerography, photocopying, microfilm*, and *recording*, or by any information storage system without permission in writing from the publishers.

Chaos Magic for Skeptics

Hell has many gates, and one of them was opened in the early morning hours of November 16-17, 2008 in Achacachi, Bolivia. During the feast of San Cristóbal, an angry mob tore eleven suspected thieves from inside a minibus, set the vehicle on fire, pushed them to a nearby stadium, beat them to death for eleven hours and set them on fire after dousing them with petrol.

Many spectators, including children, watched the demonstration of "community justice" sitting on the concrete harrows. The authorities were unable to stop the beating until police special task forces managed to rescue nine survivors in appalling physical condition. The other two had already died as a result of the severe burns inflicted. I was a witness to the lynching. And not from the stands, but embedded in the very center of horror, caught in the tumult, sucked into the maelstrom.

I was a direct witness though I was not present. On the morning of November 17, I woke up with a start, nine thousand kilometers from Achacachi, in Madrid, covered in sweat and shocked by what I had just experienced. Only very rarely had I dreamed of something so vivid, so indistinguishable from reality. But never something, not even remotely, so distressing. The feeling of disgust and restlessness blew my mind for the rest of the day. Ten years after then, disturbance still assails me when the memory emerges.

I could not understand the meaning of that. I knew, while dreaming, because in dreams we know, without further ado, that events were taking place in some town in the Bolivian highlands. But why dream of an event of these characteristics in a remote country, With such rare hyper-realistic sharpness, too! I could not relate it to any event or reading from previous days or months. I did not know nor had any relationship with Bolivians until then; no incidental, no personal, no professional relationship, of any kind. I had never traveled to Bolivia and had never planned to do so. Nothing justified my nightmare.

However, it was more than a nightmare. Not even twenty-four hours would elapse before I came across the news published on the Internet: "Brutal lynching in Achacachi; two die burned by the mob". [1]

Indeed, at around eleven o'clock on November 16, the alleged bandits had been identified and captured. At half past three in the morning of the 17th, a group set fire to the minibus in a nearby lot and shortly after the crowd, two thousand people, transferred the captives from a social headquarters where they had been interrogated to the Achacachi stadium, where the actual lynching took place. At dawn the mob stoned the police and army members who were trying to stop the slaughtering. At 10:00am, nine survivors were evacuated.

The news, spread through various media, was accompanied by some photographs: I recognized the green

---

1. http://eju.tv/2008/11/brutal-linchamiento-en-achacachi-dos-mueren-quemados-por-la-turba/

and white burned Volkswagen minibus; I did not recognize any specific face but the appearance and general clothing of the crowd, the exact number of "executed," those wounds and burns; I recognized the lot, the dusty court, and the concrete bleachers of the stadium.

I did not identify anything related to the arrest of the eleven wretches or the final rescue for a reason: that I had not dreamed of it. In my dream I saw what happened, roughly, between half past three and some indeterminate time after four. Which corresponds, in Spanish time, to the interval that goes from half past nine to ten in the morning.

I had dreamed it live.

There was, however, something wrong. A single detail that would have been enough to show that I had not been there physically. In Achacachi it did not dawn until a few minutes before six, but in my dream the sun shone in the sky all the time. How it shone in Madrid when I woke up. A very curious incongruity. A very significant incongruity.

So was it really a dream? About my geographical and physical location, I have no doubts. My body did not teleport to South America at night to return to my bed in Europe in the morning. What then, an astral travel, My "astral body" making its own decisions, eager to attend some horrifying event, flew over the Atlantic and appeared without further ado in the middle of that coven of violence as a kind of evanescent reporter? Well, let's assume such wonders can happen. But then, why did my unfolding make me witness everything in a light that does not match the darkness of the night in which the events occurred, as if he had dragged the time zone from one continent to another? No, I am also skeptical of this hypothesis. And, I have to admit, I am quite a die-hard skeptic. I don't believe in astral travel.

This all may surprise the reader. Not only because of the choice of such an unpleasant topic, a savage lynching, worth the pleonasm, although in my defence, I have to point out that I have omitted the most atrocious details; but also for starting to approach a subject like magic, by making a double and apparently contradictory confession: that of a personal experience worthy of a parapsychology memorandum and, immediately afterwards, that of my skepticism.

There is no such contradiction. Treating what is going to be discussed here and for the reader's consideration, it is convenient to make clear what we mean by skepticism and to demarcate the boundaries in which mine is framed, which is vast and not very forgiving. Borders that, moreover, have barely varied over time. Like I said, I don't believe in astral travel. Not, at least, in the extended version of a subtle body physically shedding its flesh-like sheath. Nor do I consult horoscopes, although I think that the description of my own sign is astonishingly plausible; like, I understand, it happens to almost anyone who reads the description of their own sign. I love black cats. If my head hurts, I resort to something as barely homeopathic as paracetamol. And regarding the ghosts … Okay, I find it difficult to be blunt about this, since I have met a handful of all sorts, and often very palpable. These I have experienced, albeit sporadically, always unexpectedly and, of course, far removed from that feeling of horror. Fortunately I have not received anything similar to the dream described, knock on wood, I have experienced throughout the time, I say, a series of curious phenomena related to clairvoyance, precognition or, simply, synchronicity, which, although not too extensive, is enough to question some of the certainties about the functioning of reality that should, they say, be considered unquestionable by a mentality as skeptical as mine.

Personal experience has persuaded me that it is as unscientific to attribute the causes of certain unusual events to angelic interference as it is to fate. As suspicious of fairy tales as we may be, when an event overwhelmingly and repeatedly defies the law of probability, perhaps the rational thing to do should be not to be stubborn about it but to admit that it is more sensible to accept the involvement of an ulterior motive. Although this implies an eventual challenge to our polished building of beliefs.

But note that I have alluded to questioning, not accepting new beliefs. I mean that my skepticism remains perfectly intact despite, or apart from, or perhaps thanks to my subjective encounters with the incomprehensible. This is so because I consider that the potential field of knowledge is vast, that one's own convictions must be subject to constant revision, that any "certainty" must be considered a working hypothesis and that the last word has not yet been pronounced on anything at all. And, it is difficult to venture into it, so I probably never pronounce it. That is to say, at times my skepticism is reinforced: when what provokes skepticism is precisely the recalcitrant and deeply unscientific skepticism, perhaps it should be called denialism, of others. Especially when it is accompanied by a condescending smile.

As for the other leg of the apparent contradiction, suffice it to say that this essay is not strictly about magic, but about a specific kind of magic, perhaps peculiar: chaos magic. And chaos magic is, strange as it may sound, a magic for skeptics. For skeptics, by the way, are individualists, rabidly individualistic. In fact, it is commonplace both among the ascendants of chaos magic and among reputable chaoists to hasten to declare their skepticism at the slightest opportunity they are given. Hence Robert Anton Wilson and his assertion "I don't believe anything", Grant Morrison calling himself a "tough skeptic", and so on. When they write a book or an article, they tend to pounce in the first paragraph proclaiming their disbelief with urgency, trying at all costs to avoid any reader jumping on the point and taking them for some simpletons. Is it honesty or pretense, I do not know, I can not and do not intend to decipher the convictions of others. I have enough with trying to unravel mine.

I have always been interested in border spaces, transition zones, blurred edges between a priori opposite subjects. The quarter tones between the white keys and the black keys. The interstices of reality. There is an ambiguous, misty space that harbors enormous potential for intellectual fertility, where current science, the most self-conscious art and what has traditionally been considered magic converge. The most daring visions of physicists and cosmologists, the intuition of truly visionary artists and also the philosophical concerns of less accommodating magicians wander in this territory. It is in that uncertain region of knowledge that the magic of chaos must be located. It is not surprising, then, that among its founders and practitioners there are not a few scientists and artists, some of unique talent.

How could it be otherwise, all magical currents have been daughters of their time. Chaos magic, also called pop or postmodern, with more or less sarcastic aim, arises relatively recently, in the last quarter of the 20th century and, since then, has enjoyed, and still enjoys, great prestige in the English-speaking world. Also in other countries, such as Germany or Brazil. However, its spread to this day in the rest of the world and particularly in Spain and in the Spanish-speaking sphere has been meager, limited to willful circles, although small in number, of followers, and has generated a bibliography in Spanish that we could qualify, being benevolent, as scarce. This is an astonishing void given the interest that, because of its transgressive and rabidly contemporary condition, it should arouse.

I want to add something else to this preliminary, I have decided to convey to the reader a compendium of my inquiries and reflections on the chaos magic using the first person, with an approach that we could qualify as gonzo essayism. That is because already at a very early stage of the writing it became clear to me how inappropriate it would be to approach such a subject from a distance that, in my case, could only be faked, and from a journalistic or anthropological coldness that would necessarily have to squeak. I am not a journalist or an anthropologist. I write theater and direct films, some of my works are inspired by subjects and figures, such as Aleister Crowley or Charles Howard Hinton, who will come as guest characters to the paragraphs of this dissertation, and my approach to this or any other subject will inevitably be eclectic, unacademic, and somewhat, perhaps appropriately, in this case, chaotic.

But it is not a strictly guild objection which makes a distant approach impossible. There is something else. At first I didn't know what it was. Then I realized that my case is no exception: all the magic books I have read are written in the first person. And I can see why. Perhaps it is because magic is fundamentally a point of view, a projection of meaning on the events that make up the world. Perhaps the books themselves are acts of magic. And, finally, magic is also an art form, with which this entails the implication of subjectivity.

Regarding my condition as a magician, or as a non-magician, I rely on the recommendation of Alan Moore, the famous comic book writer: you have to be careful, because it is enough for one to declare oneself a magician to be one. I think he says it from experience. And I rely too in the words of Eliphas Lévi,[2] when he warns that magic is not a profession and, also, when he enumerates the Four Powers of the magician represented in the Great Sphinx of

---

2 Lévi, É. (1992: 200) «He must have another profession than that of a magician; magic is not a trade.»

Giza: To Know, To Will, To Dare and To Keep Silent.[3] So, on this point, I will declare I am not. Of course, I am not a magician. And if I were, I would deny it. Once the presentation has been completed, it is time to get down to business.

*

In my youth, during the penultimate decade of the twentieth century, not long after the advent of chaos magic in this vale of tears, I invented a mental game whose practice caused me a very special and deeply pleasant sensation. The sea, or more specifically the location of the sea, played an important role in that game.

Perhaps because I was born in a city on the Mediterranean shores, the proximity of the sea has exerted, for as long as I can remember, a notable influence on the different layers of my conscious and unconscious mind, also rendering a valuable service to my sense of direction, as a pre-set compass. For much of my life, its eventual distance has not only caused me disorientation, but also uneasiness.

More than once, arriving by road at some town on the plateau, I was seized for a fleeting moment, by a sudden joy at mistaking the lowest strip of sky against which the houses were silhouetted with the turquoise blue of the nautical horizon. Joy that immediately turned to disappointment when I realized that I was no less than five hundred kilometers from the nearest coastline.

The mental game I have mentioned, which I could then practice effortlessly and at almost any time, unlike today, to

---

3. Lévi, É. (1992: 31)

my misfortune, consisted of unscrewing the case of the mental orientation mechanism and fumbling with its gears.

I proceeded as follows: I took a seat in a public place in the city, for example in a square, from where the sea was not visible. I sat facing the direction where I knew the sea to be, usually in the East, and I remained motionless, emptying my mind of any thought other than concentrating on the presence of the sea in that place. This was the easiest thing. Now the exciting thing happened, once I had internalized the absolute conviction or the realization of where the sea was, my imagination relocated it to another cardinal point, for example, to the North of the square, then South, then West, behind me.

Of course, the possibilities did not end here. The four basic orientations could also, sectioned by their bisectors,

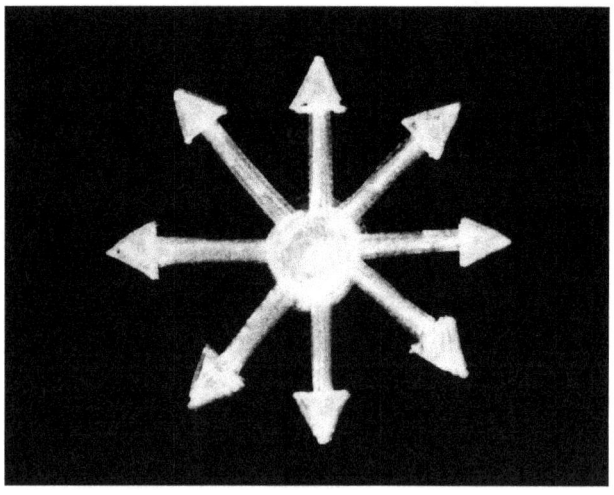

[Fig. 01]

be doubled to eight. And in a really difficult jump that required a triple somersault of concentrated, gyroscopic imagination, in all directions of three-dimensional space.

As displayed, even implicitly, in the chaosphere, the emblem of chaos magic.

Also called chaos star or chaos symbol, the chaosphere is an ideogram with a radial structure from the center of which eight arrows depart in divergent directions. There is no canonical interpretation of its meaning and I will not dare to postulate it. Different versions relate the arrows to Timothy Leary's eight-circuit model of consciousness or to the eight types of magic, in turn related to eight colors, in turn related to eight "planets",

Death magic, black, Saturn;

Sex magic, purple, Moon;

Love magic, green, Venus;

and so on.

This semantic lack of definition should not worry us. It is okay for the meaning to remain open and invite reflection. It is a condition inherent to symbols and especially appropriate in one that represents not just chaos, but the liquid heterodoxy of chaos magic.

But there is another ongoing controversy about its geometric qualities in which I do dare to intervene. It has to do with the apparent discord between name and shape. On the one hand, its name, chaosphere, refers to a spherical, three-dimensional volume, the chaos ball, the chaos bubble. But, on the other hand, its graphic expression seems to suggest a flat irradiation, in two dimensions. The attempt to get both aspects together has led to clumsy reconfigurations of the emblem, such as a shaggy ball from which eight arrows sprout in different directions in space. I have seen that drawing in some places. Even in a book by Peter J. Carroll, the egregious beacon of chaoism!

In my opinion it is a sterile stubbornness. There is no contradiction, on the contrary, assigning a three-dimensional name to a two-dimensional representation suggests the validity of the object in different dimensional reference systems and shows that the two-dimensional figure has, simultaneously, sense in itself and sense as a projection, or shadow, of a three-dimensional figure.

A three-dimensional figure that, by the way and extrapolating the geometric logic of the two-dimensional object, if built in its own space should radiate in fourteen directions and not in eight, just as it should radiate in two, back and forth, in a one-dimensional version and, may the mathematicians correct me if I am wrong, forty in four-dimensional space.

I launch a proposal, I encourage those endowed with a geometric intrepidity superior to mine to calculate, for pure amusement, the number of arrows that should bristle the chaospheric ball in successively more complex dimensional spaces. On a whim, the eight-dimensional one strikes me as especially significant.

That said, and returning to its usual representation, it is difficult to escape an instantaneous association, that of the eight-pointed star with the octagon, the regular polygon with eight vertices. And, piling on, it is interesting to go to the decipherment that mathematician and esotericist René Guénon makes of its symbolic keys:

> "From the point of view of cosmic symbolism in its spatial aspect, the quaternary shape, that is, that of the square when it comes to polygons, is naturally in relation to the four cardinal points and their various traditional correspondences. To obtain the octagonal shape, one must also consider, among the four cardinal points, the four intermediate points, which form with them a set of eight directions, those that various traditions designate as the eight winds."[4]

Mention of the winds which spills out to the foot of the page:

> "Let us note, in passing, the singular character of the expression rose of the winds, which is commonly used without paying attention to it: in Rosicrucian symbolism, Rosa Mundi and Rota Mundi were equivalent expressions, and the Rosa Mundi was represented precisely with eight rays, corresponding to the elements and the sensible qualities."[5]

Which brings us back to the cardinal rotation based meditation experiences that I was describing a few

---

4. GUÉNON, R. (1995: 206)
5. GUÉNON, R. (1995: 206, footnote). Of course by *elements* Guénon refers to fire, earth, water and air; and by *sensitive qualities* to hot, cold, dry and humid.

paragraphs ago. Just before skewing my speech into the chaosphere, I explained what I was doing. Now I will explain why I did it.

With each relocation, my perception of the square experienced a radical change, of the square, the world, and my relationship with the world. My mood was drastically altered. If the sea was in a place, it was Sunday morning; if it was in another, Friday afternoon. I could, in a matter of seconds, jump from a fateful Monday to a lazy, lazy Saturday. And no one, I hope, is going to doubt that subjective and objective reality is not the same on Monday as on Saturday. I hasten to dispel the doubts, I am not saying that it perpetuates travel in time. I don't jump into the future and into the past. They were perceptual changes intimately meshed with the emotional.

The successive perceptions of being in an altered time and place were so intense and enveloping that they bordered on the disturbing. And I achieved it with this exercise of the imagination, apparently so simple and anodyne, based on the trick of altering the position of the square with respect to the sea in order. And this is the decisive thing, to vary the spatial relationship of everything in that moment, I and my surroundings were with respect to the cardinal points, the sun and the magnetic poles of the earth; remaining static, and ecstatic. In the center of the wheel of the world, the Rota Mundi alluded to by Guénon, stirring, inverting, turning the intricate emotional and sensitive skin that connects our self with the path of sunlight and with the geomagnetic field, with the zenith and nadir of the universe.

This experience of immersion in an altered, transcendental state of consciousness, of one-with-the-cosmos, bears evident parallels with the nirvikalpa samadhi of yoga and with the oceanic feeling that after having experienced it, Romain Rolland referred to Sigmund Freud.[6]

The consequences of the exercise lasted for hours after its execution: a soft placidity, an increase in the resolution capacity and a loosening of inspiration that translated into an amazing display of creativity. Unfortunately, as I have already pointed out, it is much more difficult for me today than in my youth to carry out this particular operation of the imagination. I put the blame on neglecting the training. But we must also assume the inevitable losses that accumulating years bring, imagination is, in a sense, a muscle and, as with other muscles, exercise delays but does not prevent age from inexorably reducing its vigor. Perseverance and discipline are essential in its maintenance.

Of course there are always alternatives. I have never stopped experimenting and coming up with other methods, more appropriate to each vital circumstance, in order to

---

6. According to Freud's account, Rolland understood that in this «feeling of eternity», perceived by him and by millions of people, the ultimate source of religiosity would lie. In turn, Freud, who had not experienced it, denies «the primary nature of such a feeling», given the inability of man to «intuit his relationship with the external world through a direct feeling, oriented from the beginning for this purpose.» And he attributes it to a reminiscence of the early ego sense, typical of infants, when man has not yet learned to discern «the interior (belonging to the self) from the exterior (originated in the world).» *Vid* FREUD, S. (1997: 24-30)

continue extracting brimming buckets from the unfathomable well of imagination. Methods that, now, not like then, I know could be described as magical.

When I sat in that square to rotate the world around me, I was unaware that I was probably doing magic. I was unaware that the tips of my fingers were touching what in chaos magic is called the gnosis state, the altered state of consciousness focused on a single idea, essential to perform magical work. Now I suspect that was exactly what I was doing. And even more: by creating my own systems, by not adjusting to more or less pre-established systems, vicarious systems, by enhancing my creativity from the use of my own creativity, in a kind of feedback loop of creativity, I was perhaps practicing a very specific kind of magic. It was probably chaos magic.

Before entering its chaoist side, let's stop at a primary question: what do we mean when we say magic. Magic without adjectives. Are we talking about extracting rabbits from top hats, levitating stones, or conferring with the sleeping gods of civilizations buried under the sands of time, It is clear that we are not talking about sleight of hand. Nor about religion. What are we talking about then, Does this magic exist?

Rare would be the reader who, having reached this point, did not expect a categorical confirmation or a resounding denial of that question. And, given the choice, it better be the affirmative answer. As I do not aspire to disappoint expectations, and at the risk of being wrong, we must always have, I insist, the sword of a reasonable doubt hanging over our most assumed certainties; also, and especially, the chaoists, I am going to make the following assertion:

Yes. Of course.

The validity and ubiquity of magic are beyond doubt. It is enough to take a look around and fix our attention on those power acts or demonstrations that, constantly and in view of everyone, are carried out through the image, the gesture or the word. No longer ostensibly, like the Churchill's "V" sign, an idea with which Aleister Crowley sought to counter the power of the swastika and which he brought to the premier through his friends in Naval Intelligence. The casting among the American troops of fifty-two playing cards decks with the faces of the most wanted high-ranking officials of the Iraqi regime. Or the controversial opening ceremony of the Gotthard Tunnel in June 2016, but also in such a daily and widespread way that, for acclimatization, we hardly notice its magical nature: logos of large corporations, electoral slogans, institutional formalisms, the repeated use of the symbolic in any facet of human activity, be it private, political, economic, military or artistic.

Let us pay attention, for example, to the implantation that is most fascinating to me because of the almost total, and at the same time unthinking, acceptance that it arouses, regardless of time or latitude: the use of performative sentences. Something so essential for the most essential institutions of any human society and, at the same time, so connected with an idea as genuinely magical as the effective power of the word. Without metonyms: of the word itself.

It is enough that a priest or a judge, acting as vicar of a power that has been transferred to him by a higher, transcendent entity, declares us, aloud, "united" in marriage or "guilty" of a crime for the act to be perform and acquire immediate nature of truth for all legal purposes. Civil, if the sentence is pronounced by public opinion. Factually, if an angry crowd does.

Let's not make the mistake of assuming that a performative statement is just a convention. It is, yes, but in a deeper sense. Performative statements do not describe, nor do they embellish. They perform. Nobody miss the rabidly objective implications, of changes in reality, that flow from them. One word is enough to turn a life upside down. Or to put it in the right side, but to disrupt it in any case. A man declares that two individuals are united in marriage and, immediately and as a result of that declaration, those two individuals are a married couple. A judge declares that a person is guilty and, immediately and as a result of that declaration, that person is guilty. Don't tell me it doesn't sound like magic to you. It turns out that it surely is.

*

Performativity is the most palpable demonstration that, apart from our unavoidable interactions with the physical world, we live immersed in a symbolic ocean as real and determining as matter, but often as unnoticed as water for fish. In this regard, it is appropriate to recall the sniper sequence in the film *The Phantom of Liberty*, in which Luis

Buñuel[7] and Jean-Claude Carrière shake our discernment with astonishing acuity not devoid of black humor: Bernard Levasseur, a man armed with a rifle, stationed in a tall office building, carries out an indiscriminate shootout against Parisian passersby. After killing a few (and a pigeon) he is arrested by the police. A trial is held. The court finds him guilty and sentences him to death. Then a gendarme frees Levasseur from his handcuffs and a lawyer lights him a cigarette. Levasseur leaves the courtroom smoking, calmly walks down the courthouse stairs, signs a couple of autographs for some young ladies who are waiting for him by the door, and leaves.

The difference between pronouncing a spell dressed in a tunic before a magic altar, or dressed in a robe or a chasuble in a different environment, but also arranged according to a ritual conceived to act as a symbolic resonance box of what happens there, the difference, I say, that will be wielded by those who contest the magical quality of the second case, is that, in this case, the higher and transcendent entity that invests the officiant with authority has a physical expression that no one disputes. Matters of faith are ultimately bound by legality; and, no matter how abstract the notions of Justice or Law may be at times, legality is based on a solid coercive basis against which it can be physically painful to collide, and which responds, when asked, to the name of *State*. In other words, we can linger as long as we want, but the judge's gavel awaiting at the end of a path of contempt will lead us

---

7. SILBERMAN, S. (producer) and Buñuel L. (director). (1974). *Le fantôme de la liberté*. France: Greenwich Film Productions.

directly to the cold and iron handcuffs of an agent and to the cold and iron bars of a dungeon. In contrast, it is not so clear what kind of batteries power a wizard's wand.

However, this difference, decisive for some, questionable for others, is preceded by a prior truth, which is not its consequence: the conviction that the performative act is real. That's where the magic works. Regardless of whether or not the contracting parties are thinking about the practical complications of their future divorce while the priest orders not to separate what God has united, or whether or not the defendant is pondering the economic or criminal consequences of his sentence, who knows, may be more concerned about the social damage it will cause to his professional prestige, no one questions, except in certain circumstances, that the words of the priest or the judge become fact. Both the mind of the talker and the receiver are at that moment operating on a strictly shared symbolic plane, as remote from the rest of the world as if they were inside a magic circle of protection.

Magic consists to a large extent, although said like that it may sound alarming, in the influence on the minds, one's own and/or those of others. Except for some external interference, a natural catastrophe, a mechanical breakdown or a hereditary disease, our entire life consists of, and depends on, the interaction with the intersubjective network established with others, with their perception and with the decisions that they take and that affect us: to vote, or not, in our favor in a contest; to be invited and go, or not, to a party; whether or not we are granted a mortgage loan, and so on. And in 90% that decision making happens at an unconscious level. We fall in love with someone because we like him/her, we meet in a restaurant and order cod because we feel like it. We are aware of this and each of these decision-making seems to show that we are endowed with free will. But we are also completely unable to explain why we like it or why we feel like it. The unconscious decides for us. And their internal motives, psychic, metabolic and, inevitably, inadvertent external influences join and overlap.

Magic distorts, amplifies, disturbs the perception of oneself and others. This implies a change in reality, understood as the sphere of our perceptions. This is how the political, media and religious powers proceed. We can turn our backs on them and ignore them, but we will continue to be the object of their influence. What do they say about politics, That we can disregard it, but it has no intention of disregarding us. What do they say about the devil, That its success lies in convincing us that he does not exist.

With this I do not intend to contribute to the propagation of conspiracy presumptions related to the celebration of pagan rites and invocations to goats and unknown superiors on the part of the leaders of the powers-that-be, although it would not be difficult considering the amount of theories in this regard, to which some famous cinematographic depiction is not unrelated[8] and of real and very blatant examples of the political use of magic. There we find, observing the landmarks of the Dark Side, the

---

8. For instance: KUBRICK, S. (producer and director). (1999). *Eyes wide shut*. U.K./U.S.A.: Warner Bros.

occult idiosyncrasy of National Socialism or, even more clearly, the use that François Duvalier, Papa Doc, made of voodoo, and Tonton Macoute machetes, to subjugate the Haitians.

No, it is not necessary to resort to such blatant cases. It is enough to remember that magical thinking has never been and can never be removed from the deepest roots of the human mind; that, consequently, to a greater or lesser degree we are all susceptible to letting ourselves be guided by it, especially when we graze in herds. This susceptibility is a very powerful tool and, in the same way that most of us operate the remote control of the television without knowing the details of its mechanism, the hands that use this tool do not require specific knowledge beyond its willingness to manipulate consciences.

Against these assertions it will be objected that seduction, marketing and persuasion do not exert their influence through any magical procedure. This objection is based on the fact that no phenomenon capable of being elucidated through scientific reasoning, be it now or in an uncertain tomorrow, that is, in the end, no phenomenon at all should be classified under the heading of magical phenomenon. However, this is a misinterpretation of what magic is and means. This is an understandable misunderstanding, given the many sediments of prejudice that have built up on the issue over time. And not only thanks to the contribution of the deniers.[9]

At best, acceptance of its effectiveness has been inextricably linked to its disapproval. Magic has been accused of immorality by its persecutors in the same way that chaos magic has been accused of immorality by practitioners of other magics, who, in addition to considering it irreverent, brand it as magic of results due to its utilitarianism lacking of spirituality. As if, in turn, the accusers, wrapped in the oriflammes of a higher good, did not also seek the achievement of results. The virtue adduced by magicians since time immemorial, abstinence, meditation, etc., is not, at bottom, and at this point we agree with Aleister Crowley, more than a way of concentrating the mind in the state of a single thought. In other words, virtue is a tool at the service of efficiency.

Ok, but manipulating people, wasn't that bad, indeed, it is. But manipulating is one thing and influencing is another. Convincing a girl not to give in to frustration, build her self-confidence, and persist in pursuing her aspirations is good. Setting off a blue whale challenge to drive dozens or

---

9 "Currently, the magician is in charge of public relations, propaganda, market research, sociological surveys, advertising, information, counter information and misinformation, censorship, espionage operations and even cryptography (this science was, during the 16th century, a branch of magic) [...] Historians concluded without reason that magic had disappeared with the arrival of "quantitative science". This has only replaced a part of magic, prolonging their dreams and their goals, resorting to technology [...] By maintaining an operational function, Sociology, applied Psychology and Psychosociology represent, nowadays, the direct continuation of Renaissance magic." CULIANU, I. P. (1999: 149)

hundreds of teenagers to suicide is decidedly monstrous.[10] On the moral ground, magic is in no way different from the influence that, as I have said, we exert on our fellows and receive from them permanently. Could it be that we could not influence, our mere existence implies an influence on others. Once the inevitable is assumed, our duty is to channel that influence towards goals that are laudable or, at the very least, not harmful to others.

Let's turn to the most venerable of the classics on influencing others, Dale Carnegie's book *How to Win Friends and Influence People*: What do we find in those pages, paeans to emotional blackmail, wicked hypnotism tricks, scopolamine drops discreetly poured into other people's glasses? By no means, quite the opposite: a repeated call to put ourselves in the place of the other, to listen to them with sincere interest, to discover how we can be more useful and make life pleasant for others. In short, to behave empathically, generously and kindly with others. That influence, the famous "Give, and it shall be given unto you" in Luke 6:38, is in short the one that has the greatest benefits to bring us. That Charles Manson adopted *How to Win Friends* as a bedside book is

---

10. Former Russian Psychology student Philipp Budeikin created the online game Blue Whale Challenge with the macabre intention of "cleaning up" society. Although the magnitude of the damage caused is difficult to calculate exactly, it is estimated that its activation on the Vkontakte social network in 2013 and its subsequent dissemination through platforms in other countries have caused more than a hundred teenage suicides worldwide, in addition to countless unsuccessful attempts and self-harm. In November 2016, Budeikin was arrested by the police and, in July 2017, sentenced by the Tobolsk court (Siberia) to a controversial sentence of three years and four months in prison.

nothing more than a one-off fatality. If we had to establish a moral precept to guide the decisions of a magician, I can only think of the following: behave yourself, respect people and do not trample the lives of others. It is clear that this applies equally to magic and non-magic.

To reinforce my eloquence, I propose to read carefully the following paragraph by the chaoist Jaq D. Hawkins:

> "An old formula which was popular to quote a few decades ago was that magic used for healing was white magic, while magic used for selfish ends was black magic, and therefore evil."[11]

And once you have read the passage, reread it, but replace the word "magic" with "drinking water", "government budget" or "power of conviction." It is not worth dwelling on a debate, the moral one, which is exhausted before walking five steps. So let's get on with the substantive thing: what is magic?

My favorite definition of magic, for elegant, synthetic and enlightening, is enunciated by Aleister Crowley in his famous treatise *Magick in Theory and Practice*, where, with the term Magick, he alludes to his own magical system, or Thelemic magic; but that does not mean that the definition ceases to be relevant to magic in general.

Crowley says that the Magick is:

> "The Science and Art of causing Change to occur in conformity with Will."

---

11. HAWKINS, J. D. (1996: 83)

To which he adds:

"Illustration: It is my Will to inform the World of certain facts within my knowledge. I therefore take "magical weapons," pen, ink, and paper; I write "incantations", these sentences, in the "magical language," i.e. that which is understood by the people I wish to instruct; I call forth "spirits," such as printers, publishers, booksellers, and so forth, and constrain them to convey my message to those people. The composition and distribution of this book is thus an act of

MAGICK

by which I cause Changes to take place in conformity with my Will."[12]

Pens, ink, paper, booksellers … Does this mean that phoning the nearest pizzeria to have a quattro formaggi brought home is an act of magic, Good question. The answer is no. Telephoning the pizzeria does not generate a change in reality, only the activation of a chain of predetermined maneuvers, oven, collection, transport, etc., that does not occur according to our Will, the True Will referred to by Crowley, , but to a less elevated physiological need: perhaps gluttony or perhaps appetite. The act of magic was performed, in any case, by the person who once

---

12 Crowley A. (1994: xiii)

enriched himself by putting into practice the idea of delivering pizzas at home. I take this opportunity to make a point: I consider unfair the somewhat secondary role in which Crowley is usually relegated in the cast of illustrious predecessors of chaos magic compared, for example, with the prominent place that chaoists always assign to Austin Osman Spare. The magic of chaos owes as much to Crowley's eclecticism and formidable pragmatic vision as to the stealth technique developed by Spare. If not more. End of subsection. [13]

*

Magic is a matter of faith. But is something other than that, you can believe that magic does not exist. You can also believe that there is nothing else, such as love, potato chips or the entire universe. You can take for granted that the cosmos is not an illusion or, on the contrary, that it is not an objective reality. You can take for granted that there are more subjects apart from the self or, conversely, embrace solipsism. All of these are beliefs. After all, all knowledge is

---

13. Tim Maroney's text «Six voices on Crowley» serves to illustrate this detachment to Master Therion, bordering on ingratitude. Giving voice to a fictional "Chaoist", Maroney synthesizes the reasons for distancing: «I'm tired of Crowley. [...] I'm suspicious of his system; way too regimented, way too hierarchical. Crowley contributed to magic, but so have other people. We've learned a lot in the last century about real freedom and sexual liberation, and a Victorian master-of-the-passions approach would be a step backward. Crowley had a lot of hang-ups; I'd rather work a system more relevant to my life.» METZGER, Richard (2014: 182)

intrinsically axiomatic and is based on faith, that is, on belief without verification.

Even mathematics is supported by unprovable axioms. For example: that all right angles are equal to each other or that a line segment can extend indefinitely in a straight line. Most of these axioms have remained unchanged throughout history, but not all: the revision of the fifth postulate of Euclid,[14] in force for more than two thousand years, took place in the 19th century to non-Euclidean geometry, a subversion that happily broadened our understanding of space.

In short, the human being proposes provisional models to explain the universe, that will be all the more useful, the more closely they adjust to the reality that we perceive, the better they demonstrate their predictability. And we legitimately assume that this is occurring with increasing precision. But a map is not the territory and a model of the universe, precise as it may be, is not the universe. Amazed by the surprising accuracy with which mathematics describes, and still predicts, the laws of nature, thinkers have wondered for centuries whether, as Pythagoras posited, mathematics itself is inherent in nature, that is, whether the universe is mathematical, whether it is made of numbers. Or if, simply,

---

14. The fifth postulate of Euclid said the following: if a line affects two lines making the internal angles of the same side smaller than two right angles, the two lines prolonged indefinitely will meet on the side where the angles are smaller than two right angles.

we are skillful inventors who have had the providential luck to come up with such a fine-tuned descriptive instrument.[15]

In a TV interview,[16] British actor and director Ricky Gervais, questioned about his (non) religious beliefs, made a well-argued defense of his atheism. However, at one point he made an assertion that, despite receiving applause from the public and being praised by his opponent in the debate, the show's host, a practicing and declared Catholic? It was clearly untenable from the same skeptical logic behind the rest of his dissertation. Gervais claimed that if we destroyed the holy books, after a thousand years they would not resurface as they were. We would have different holy books. But if we destroyed the science books, after a thousand

---

15. "It is often heard that successive theories get closer and closer to the truth. Apparently, this type of generalizations allude not to the solution of puzzles nor to the concrete predictions derived from a theory, but rather to its ontology, that is, to the correspondence between the entities with which the theory populates nature and what it is "really there." [...] I think there is no way to reconstruct expressions like "really there" that is independent of theories. At first, the idea of ??a correspondence between the ontology of a theory and its "real" counterpart in nature seems illusory to me. Furthermore, as a historian, I am struck by the implausibility of that point of view. I have no doubt, for example, that Newtonian mechanics improves on Aristotle's and that Einstein's does the same with Newton's as a puzzle-solving tool. But in its succession I am unable to see a coherent direction of ontological development. On the contrary, in some important respects, though not all at all, Einstein's general theory of relativity is closer to Aristotle's than either of them is to Newton's". KUHN, T. S. (2006: 348).
16. February 2017, The Late Show with Stephen Colbert, CBS. The video fragment with the aforementioned intervention can easily be found on the Internet under the heading "Ricky Gervais And Stephen Go Head-To-Head On Religion".

years they would come back, because the same problems would have the same result.

It is a reckless assertion, indeed, based on a slippery distinction between what he considers fictitious and contingent, religion, belief, and real and necessary, science, not belief. And although it seems that the Japanese mathematics of the Edo[17] period would come to agree with him, there is nothing, absolutely nothing to prove that a restart from scratch of human thought after a total cultural hecatomb should inevitably lead us to re encounter with the same scientific models that we have been building so far. It is possible to imagine that science would resurface from different axioms and focus its attention on issues that, for us, at this moment, immersed as we are in our own paradigm, are completely unimaginable, which would generate different models from the ones we now have but equally useful in describing reality. Reality of those people. Of whatever it was that by then was taken for reality. We don't even know what questions they would ask themselves. A paradigm can be born from the germ contained in a question, but all questions are born from its own paradigm.

As for religion, at least one piece of information should put us on our guard, the irrefutable coincidence of founding

---

17. Only in appearance since, although it is true that during Edo isolation period (1603-1868) Japan produced a mathematics independent of the rest of the world with which it obtained some identical and almost simultaneous results to those of mathematics, it should also be noted that Japan did not sprout out from nowhere in 1603. They had been influenced by Chinese mathematics up to that date, and no clean slate was made with previously acquired knowledge.

myths in so many religions that arose within distant cultures and without mutual contact. The profusion of concomitances throughout the length and breadth of the planet, such as the celestial location of the gods, the primordial chaos, the race of giants, the great flood and the god who dies and rises, to name just a few, denotes, even discarding divine dictation, an underlying and universal need in psychology, sustained over time and common to all human beings.

On the other hand, science, what we now understand as such, is born from singularity. Perhaps, if the Persians had given to the edge of the sword the members of the Ionian school before they opened their mouths, twenty-eight centuries later and to the exasperation of Gervais we would still be waiting for another Thales of Miletus to take the first step on the path of the scientific speculation.

The inevitability of scientific postulates stems from the widespread but erroneous notion of cumulative progress based on successive falsification of theories and, say, linear self-refinement. But, as Thomas S. Kuhn showed in *The Structure of Scientific Revolutions*, what actually occurs is an erratic journey along a contingent itinerary of successive substitutions of some paradigms by others. Only *a posteriori* does the rewriting of textbooks create the impression that progress has been linear.[18] The new paradigms are not based so much on evident empirical improvements as on intuitions, sometimes intuitions of such a purely aesthetic aspect as

---

18. KUHN, T. S. (2006: 276-280)

the beauty of an equation and the Platonic desire that that beauty corresponds to the truth.

In their earliest genesis, the new paradigms are thus sustained by acts of faith. It is the subsequent consolidation of a new successful paradigm, more by generational renewal of the scientific community than by conversion of its members, which provides the methodological framework. In which the new theoretical contributions will be revealed as more useful for the description of reality, at the same time as, we must not forget, it will mask previous knowledge, until, of course, the advent of a new crisis and a subsequent paradigm shift.

As we said, magic is also a matter of faith. But not just one. Magic is far from being a monolithic and uniform thought sustained over time. Throughout the centuries it has also projected its own models and has generated, or, rather, it has generated at the same time as it has fed on, successive world views.

The classification that Frater U:.D:. Ralph Tegtmeier's magic name, once a chaos magic practitioner and, later, of something called Pragmatic Magic, made up of four magical paradigms: spiritual, energetic, psychological, and informational. This account can be found in many places and is also collected by Patrick Dunn in his book Postmodern magic: the Art of Magic in the Information Age. I will expose it in an abbreviated way:[19]

---

19. DUNN, P. (2005: 26-34)

I- The spiritual paradigm:

It assumes the existence of divinities and spiritual entities to which the magician orders, through elaborate ceremonies of invocation or evocation, the fulfillment of a wish.

It is the oldest magical paradigm, the one that has lasted the longest, by far, the most widespread on the planet and also in popular culture. Owed to shamans, Elizabethan magicians like John Dee, New York neurosurgeons in low hours like Dr. Strange or druids like Merlin, his Creation Spell is my favorite:

"Anál nathrach, orth' bháis's bethad, do chél dénmha."

(Even if it was a true 6th century Welsh spell instead of an invention from the *Excalibur* movie,[20] it would still be magnificent.)

II- The energy paradigm:

It postulates the existence of energies or powers of a different sort from those known to science, capable of being manipulated by the magician in order to cause changes in physical reality.

It is the type of magic that, since the eighteenth century, illusionists, performers of stage magic, pretend to control for the solace of their audience. It also includes Franz Anton Mesmer's animal magnetism, Reiki's universal life energy and

---

20. BOORMAN, J., DRYHURST, M., EISENSTEIN, R. A., GROSS, E. F. (producers) and BOORMAN, J. (director). (1981). *Excalibur*. U.K./U.S.A.: Orion Pictures.

Wilhelm Reich's orgone. Eliphas Lévi, Alphonse Louis Constant's pseudonym, the most famous 19th century occultist, wrote in 1854 about his astral light that it "is projected by the gaze, by the voice, by the thumbs and by the palms of the hands."[21]

III- The psychological paradigm:

He assigns to the entities and energies mentioned above a purely psychic existence, that is, not external to the magician, but a product of his own mind. Though once generated they acquire a certain autonomy. Which is still admirable.

Aleister Crowley, who in his insatiable appetite for exploitative paradigms. Perhaps we should begin to refer to him as a metamagus, who had at least one eye on the spiritual paradigm and another on the psychological one. He contributed in the 1920s his bit to the sponsorship of this, showing a remarkable practical sense when affirming that "we may consider all beings as part of ourselves, but it is more convenient to regard them as independent. Maximum convenience is our canon of Truth."[22]

---

21. Lévi É. (1992: 188)
22. CROWLEY, A. (1994: 227)

IV- The informational paradigm

Or the cybernetics model, in the terminology proposed by Phil Hine [23]:

> It conceives reality as a semiotic web, a network of symbols not subject to the rule of matter, energy and spacetime, although closely linked to them. By acting symbolically, the magician operates in that semiotic web, software, causing changes in its structure that in turn also alter the physical reality, hardware.

> Patrick Dunn, author of the book that collects this classification of paradigms and practitioner of the informational model, wrote in 2005: "I Believe the semiotic web is the substance of Ultimate reality. [If reality] is symbolic in nature, then manipulating symbol systems manipulates the semiotic web, and therefore manipulates reality. Scientific explanations stop before attempting to find meaning. Only art and magic can explore meaning, and I think the reason is that both art and magic manipulate, coerce, shape, and coax meaning out of the hopelessly tangled mishmash of Mind."[24]

I have dated the four quotes that I have associated with each paradigm, 6th century, mid-19th century, interwar period of the 20th century, early 21st century, to highlight

---

23. HINE, P. (2009: 86)
24. DUNN, P. (2005: 36)

the symptomatic correlation that the flourishing of each magical paradigms, spiritual, energetic, psychological and informational, maintains with its respective Zeitgeist.

Surely it is not due to chance that during Antiquity, Middle Ages and Renaissance, centuries of incontestable faith in disembodied beings, angels and demons, and in their influence on worldly events, the magical paradigm was the spiritual one. After the Industrial Revolution and the discovery of electromagnetism, when the world embraced Positivism, the magical paradigm became based on energies. That as a result of the shock caused by Psychoanalysis to the ideas assumed until then about the human mind, the paradigm will become psychological. And that, in the age of the Internet, smartphones, A.I. and Big Data, magic understands reality as an interconnected network of data and becomes a way, perhaps a bit extravagant, of dealing with information.

This correlation could be interpreted as the attempt of magic to legitimize itself in the hegemonic belief system of each period. But, more plausibly, also as the verification that magic is not and has never been a blank verse in relation to the rest of human areas of knowledge and has been subject, like them, to changes in the general epistemological field; and also contributing, in turn and to some extent, to these changes. Nor has art been oblivious to social changes and scientific advances. All human culture is interrelated.

So we have four magical paradigms. Sometimes they appear in their pure state, in others overlapping. They are not necessarily mutually exclusive, Crowley's eclecticism was a notable example of this? But what I am now interested in emphasizing is what they have in common, despite their notable differences. The essential axiomatic beliefs on which all magic rests, so to speak. They are three.

First axiom:
Reality is not such.
What we understand by reality is a realm of illusion. There is a more real reality hidden behind it. The description of the nature of that other reality will depend, as we have seen, on our ascription to one or another paradigm.

Second axiom:
Consciousness is a brake.
A thunderous coffee pot full of prejudices and conditioning, whose noise prevents us from seeing both what is on the other side of the veil of illusions, a spider web that the Hindus call Veil of Maya, and inside ourselves. All magical currents propose their own methods to silence that noise and reach an altered-higher-state of consciousness. An ecstasy, a metaphysical state. A gnosis, for the chaoists.

Third axiom:
It is possible to alter the apparent reality using a shortcut.
That is, moving the threads of reality hidden behind appearances. Only by entering the altered state of

consciousness, alluded to in the second axiom, will we be in a position to manipulate these threads.

This brief outline of the theoretical foundations of magic serves to disprove, at least, one of the prejudices that weigh on it, that of its alleged acausality. All magics are causal by definition. They all conceive of some kind of causal mechanism that connects the magician's will with the effect produced. Things, in magic, don't just happen. They occur because the magician orders the execution of a work to an entity endowed with the power to execute it or because he manipulates energies, powers or symbols that cause a transformation. That is, he extends his will in action and that act has consequences. Another thing is that, in the view of a lay observer, this causality does not fit within an empirical framework of demonstration and that, therefore, the eventual results are attributed to chance. But acausality, as a concept, is inappropriate for magical praxis.

However, apart from praxis, the psychological and informational paradigms are aware of the news about acausality that has been coming from outside the realm of magic during the last century. Concepts such as Jungian synchronicity, quantum mechanics or chaos theory have questioned, more or less radically, our deterministic view of cause and effect. They have shown us that reality is not as simple as we thought and have proposed other forms of determinism.

The line that separates causal from acausal when dealing with synchronicities, subatomic particles, or complex systems is not as well drawn as we thought. And it's not clear that it will ever be. That is, despite the attempts of science to unravel the root causes of some phenomena, the suspicion that their indeterminacy and unpredictability are not apparent, that is, the reflection of an eventual technical inability to clarify them, which would be epistemic, but intrinsic to its nature, and ontological. It is a suspicion that if it does not end up establishing itself sooner or later as a certainty, it does have signs of remaining in force for a long time.

We could affirm, therefore, that acausality, indeterminacy and chaos are in the world, not in magic. The claim of magic is to provide meaning, causality and order in a presumably chaotic world. Similar to how art does it. In a transparent, deterministic world, perfectly delineated by divine design or Newton's laws, chaos entered the equation only as a primal myth. But in a new state of affairs, magic had to take up the gauntlet.

And the gauntlet was taken up by Peter J. Carroll and Ray Sherwin in 1976 when, according to legend, they met in Deptford (London) and created chaos magic.

Both Carroll and Sherwin were refractory to the dogmatism and traditional hierarchy of occult organizations and declared themselves heirs to the Austin Osman Spare's Zos Kia cult. In 1978 they published an advertisement in *The New Equinox*, the magazine of thelemic magic that they edited, with the aim of recruiting members for a new non-hierarchical organization that would fuse thelemic magic with Tantra, Zos and Tao. The result was Illuminates of Thanateros (IOT), an order that was later influenced by Discordianism and which prominent figures such as William

S. Burroughs, Timothy Leary and Robert Anton Wilson joined.

As is often the case in organizations, whether they are proclaimed hierarchical or not, history persists in disillusioning us, showing us the impossibility that, one way or another, not all of them end up being so, IOT also suffered splits and both Sherwin, first, like Carroll, later, they left the group. But what interests us here is not so much the incidental chronicle of human adventures as the conceptual contributions, truly novel, of chaos magic.

The most important of all, the most disruptive, is the meta-paradigm.

But before approaching it, we must pause to clarify concepts or we will end up dangerously entangled in a web of false homonyms. As soon as one enters the reading of texts on chaos magic, one will detect that the use of the term "paradigm" borders on the abusive.

Let's do a brief review. On one hand we have a primordial paradigm on which all magic is based, or Great Paradigm, which I have not presented as such but divided into three axioms:

A.   Reality is not such.
B.   Consciousness is a brake.
C.   By altering this (B) we can generate changes in that (A).

On the other hand, we have the enumeration of magical paradigms that claim to encompass all the successive types of magic, necessarily framed within the Great Paradigm and

that, in fact, describe the Zeitgeist of different cultural stages of civilization:
1. Spiritual.
2. Energy.
3. Psychological.
4. Informational.

We also have the famous meta-paradigm, characteristic of chaos magic, which I have not yet explained. I will develop this point later.

And finally, we must be cautious: this "finally" is provisional, we have the enumeration of magical paradigms in which the magic of chaos is specifically framed. Exposed and described by Carroll in his book *Liber Null & Psychonaut*,[25] it consists of the following six models:

1. The Chao-etheric Paradigm.
2. Probability Manipulation.
3. Morphic Field Theory.
4. Observer Created Universe.
5. The Holographic Universe.
6. Higher Dimensionality.

This last enumeration consists, approximately and without being completely limited to it, in the unfolding and detailing of the informational paradigm. Let's examine each point.

---

25. DUNN, P. (2005: 36)

1- "The Chao-etheric Paradigm"

Our reality is an island of order surrounded by an indeterministic and chaotic ocean of ether, not ruled by causal rules. We, human beings, even being the best organized structures within that disorder, are also infiltrated by that same chaos that permeates everything, which allows us to glimpse it and act as potential agents of change.

Beyond presenting an eloquent description of the universe, his translation into a tabloid headline would be: The primal chaos is still in force! and of a sympathetic link between consciousness and chaos based on a kind of consanguinity. Carroll does not provide, for the moment, any clue as to how the magician could or should interact with that ether to cause changes in reality.

2- "Probability Manipulation"

Carroll refers us to Heisenberg's uncertainty principle, the uncertain, probabilistic nature of matter at the subatomic level, and the determining role that consciousness plays in its configuration: the state of a particle is materialized at the moment it is observed.

Carroll himself warns that this paradigm is a more modest version of the first. In fact it is a reformulation in quantum terms. I would describe it as its functional, and scientist version, because the chaoetheric paradigm presents us the what. and the manipulation of probabilities, the how. Although it is a fairly general how.

In the first place, it is not clear that my interaction with matter at the quantum level has to unleash consequences at a higher level, perceivable in the ordinary sphere. Second, it is not even clear that I can establish a conscious, deliberate, and useful interaction with subatomic particles, with which I no doubt interact all the time, but unconsciously, unintentionally, and surely unproductively. Thirdly, if I could, it is also not clear that my interaction was much different from storming blindfolded into the control room of a particle accelerator, brandishing a wand like someone shaking a feather duster, in order to hit the right switches that can activate an interesting atomic reaction. In other words: maybe Mr. Carroll does; but I personally would not know very well what to do with a handful of loose electrons.

3- "Morphic Field Theory"

This controversial theory, formulated by the biologist Rupert Sheldrake, raises the possibility that all events in the universe, both those linked to living beings and inanimate matter, are associated with intangible fields of pure information that, thanks to their resonance, extend across the entire length and breadth of the universe a network of pure information that helps shape subsequent events. That is, when an event occurs for the first time, the crystallization of a mineral, an animal behavior, etc., it necessarily generates a morphic field that will contribute, without restrictions of time or distance, to a greater ease of reproduction of that same event.

I will give an example: a cold Homo erectus lit by a kind of providential inspiration rubs a stick against a wood on a bed of dry leaves and with tenacity and effort, learns to make a fire. Immediately a morphic field is generated, "the morphic field of making fire by rubbing two sticks", that affects the behavior of other Homo erectus individuals that inhabit distant continents. Before long, we have hominids who have never made contact with each other making fire all over the planet. And more and more expertly, as having absorbed by infused science the skill of an experience that was not their own. Some experiments, for example with mice learning to navigate mazes in distant laboratories, seem to suggest that the theory is not entirely wrong.[26]

This flow of information typical of morphic resonance, immediate and alien to the customary channels of transmission, inevitably recalls certain paranormal phenomena of ESP type ("Extrasensory Perception"), such as clairvoyance, in which the intelligence of distant events it is obtained by incantation. In fact, according to Carroll, the theory of morphic fields is a perfect explanation of most of these phenomena, of all of them as long as, also according to him, we leave precognition aside.

My vision of Achacachi events, for example, could very well be understood as the reception of a morphic resonance. On one hand, we would have a disturbance that was already

---

26. Although everything continues to remain in the field of suggestion. Morphic resonance should not be discarded entirely, but neither should it be viewed with less caution than we would use when considering a phenomenon like the *Hundredth monkey effect*, a phenomenon somewhat discredited, to put it mildly, as it is not reliably demonstrated that history of monkeys telepathically prompting themselves to wash apples conformed to observable facts.

riding on waves, the lynching of Achacachi was the ninth that took place in Bolivia that year. Which could, perhaps, increase its power. On the other hand, a receptivity as particularly sensitive as the state of sleep, free from the sieve of consciousness; and on the other, a remarkably clear and coherent flow of information. Too neat and exact, and coincident in time, to be attributed to chance or the eventual quantum reverberation of a few stray photons. But also suggesting at the same time, by means of a significant distortion, the incongruity of the night sun. My vision did not result from direct access to the facts. However this was possible from a mediate access, because what it had access to the trace of the events in the morphic field. Hence, my dream recomposition completed the information received with traces of the light conditions of my real location, just as we fluently include ambient noises or somatic sensations in the plot of our dreams.

4- "Observer Created Universe"

There is only what we perceive and what we do not perceive does not exist. Our Will generates reality, that reality that we perceive. Therefore, Will and Perception are two words that designate the same thing. If something we want does not materialize, it will be because it was not a wish emanating from our true will, but just a failed wish. Carroll also links this paradigm to quantum indeterminacy by reminding us that "it is the actual act of willed perception or measurement which actually creates events." Measurement precedes existence.²⁷

The observer created universe paradigm is a suspiciously solipsistic and tautological approach. If I don't get what I want it is because I didn't really want, then I really only want what I really want. And with all due respect to Mr. Carroll, a bit puerile. Apart from my resounding rejection of insinuations that point me out as responsible for lynchings and all kinds of calamities, for the mere fact of imagining their existence. The irrefutable human inclination towards sadism exceeds my inventiveness. This paradigm is not only, in the first place instance, a mere repetition of probability manipulation and, consequently, also of the chaoetheric paradigm. It is again the well-known influence that the observer exerts on quantum reality when observing it, the well-known wave function collapse.²⁸ In addition, its solipsistic approach, inevitably leads it to incongruity. Since, unlike quantum paradigms, it does not even admit the objective reality of subatomic particles. They are only the product of our Will/Perception, so it makes no sense that we intend to exert our influence on them. Determining their a posteriori state as if they were influenceable but independent objects and perhaps even pre-existing ones. And had we not agreed that measurement preceded existence?

---

27. CARROLL, P. J. (1987:195)

28. Physicists refer to *wave function collapse* as the instantaneous change in a particles system state when some part of that system is observed.

5- "The Holographic Universe"

The universe is a hologram and our reality is a projection. Everything, from the largest to the smallest, is connected to everything. And furthermore, as quantum entanglement suggests, it is a simultaneous connection of an immediacy emancipated from distance. The transmission of energy has speed limits imposed by Einsteinian physics. But not pure information, because it is neither matter nor energy. Synchronicity, and not causality, is the way in which this higher, holographic reality puts the matter and energy of our virtual world in order.

6- "Higher Dimensionality"

Carroll's favorite paradigm. Nothing indicates that our universe has to be limited to the four dimensions that we perceive, three space plus time. The existence of a single additional dimension, if not several or many, would solve not a few enigmas so far inscrutable from a four-dimensional perspective: weak interaction CP-symmetry violation, certain vacuum properties, psychokinesis...

According to this worldview, three-dimensional space is an inconceivably thin slice of a much larger universe, where energy, matter and information can move in unsuspected ways through dimensions that our senses do not have access to and reappear or exert influence on distant areas of our spacetime. Thus, the cases of indeterminacy and acausality that we observe would be no more than discrete manifestations of a causality that occurred in higher dimensions.

Although I have considered it fair to refer to the six points, personally, as my comment on the fourth paradigm will have already hinted, Carroll's classification does not convince me too much. I think it is redundant and unnecessarily wordy. The six models are too coincidental. At least complementary, and regrouping into only one or two paradigms. Let me be expeditious: I'm going to rub that list with sandpaper until I leave only what I consider essential and helpful for the sake of clarity.

As I have already pointed out, Carroll himself recognizes that it is not essential to detach the second, probability manipulation, from the first, chaoetheric universe. Together with the sixth, higher dimensionality, they could form a single paradigm. A quantum paradigm.

The fourth, observer created universe, is unnecessary. Solipsism is an alibi to explain everything and not explain anything. And it inevitably leads to its own denial. So the wisest thing to do is tiptoe around it.

But we will not do it without first clarifying something: it must be recognized that as an autosuggestion method it is useful, provided it is used with moderation. For example: let's go for a walk after persuading ourselves that everything we will see on the street, sidewalks, buildings, cars, clouds, birds, people and pets, is the product of the prodigious generating power of our imagination. It is fun to lord it over as a demiurge of a small, or not so small, newly released universe. Our proud demeanor will not go unnoticed and we will soon see that passersby will address us in a strangely unusual slavish tone. But be careful because, I have already warned, it is not advisable to overreach. After passing a certain line, the unpleasant collisions will become inevitable and someone will end up slapping us. Let's take the warning seriously: get off solipsism before the first blow, because if you don't, psychosis awaits you with open arms.

We must not forget that mental disorders associated with loss of contact with profane reality constitute a not inconsiderable risk to which practitioners of magic are undoubtedly exposed.[29] Hence, precautions such as exile rituals are taken, intended to cleanse the space of entities, influences or undesirable remains before and after, as opening and closing, of any magical work. An innovative contribution of chaos magic in this regard is laughter, a universal solvent for heaviness, a healthy response to excesses of solemnity, an ally of the Antichrist according to the intriguing librarian Jorge de Burgos. Jaq Hawkins reports that IOT members have popularized its use as banishment to end rituals, noting that "it tends to clear the air remarkably well."[30]

Banishing ritual, which spiritualist magicians understand as a safeguard against the influence of annoying entities, can be easily interpreted, from a psychological or simply rationalist point of view, as a mental hygiene procedure that works by delimiting and specifying the limits of each magical experience.

---

29. "Working with Chaos entities is definitely not recommended for inexperienced magicians. [...] Serious magic is for serious magicians who have learned how to stay in control of unpredictable situation." HAWKINS, J. D. (1996: 94-95)
30 HAWKINS, J. D. (1996: 94-95)

But let's continue with Carroll's paradigms.

The third, morphic fields, the fifth, holographic universe, and the sixth, again, higher dimensionality, can also conform, in turn, a single paradigm. In this case, eminently informational.

It is no coincidence that highest dimensionality appears twice, being both quantum and informational. Because, in fact, all these paradigms are reducible to only one: the informational one, which in turn would contain the quantum one, more restricted.

The following diagram will provide us with an overview:

Note in the diagram that the Great Paradigm contains

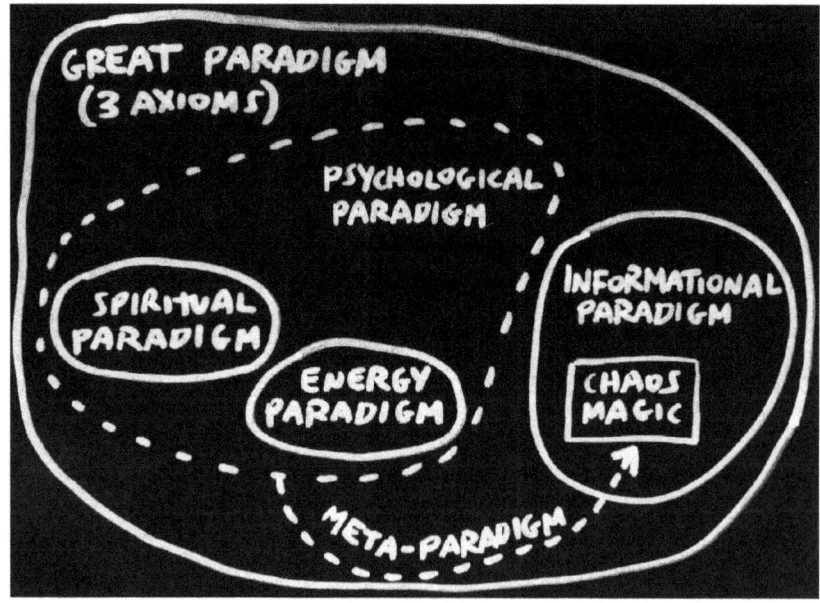

[Fig. 02]

them all and that the meta-paradigm is not shown as a set, but as a relationship between sets.

The informational paradigm, conceptual foundation of chaos magic, contains both Carroll's paradigms and their recombinations and derivations. These paradigms, those contributed by Carroll, should not, consequently, be treated individually as such, but as indications, vestiges or even pretexts of the paradigm that contains them.

In this sense, Carroll's enumeration is very useful to us because it contributes new and valuable elements that, combined with each other, enrich a model that we had dispatched as a simple semiotic web in which the magician could operate, transforming it into a powerful vision of the reality, coherent, credible and stimulating in a superlative degree. The master key of this worldview is a concept that emerged in the field of Psychology at the beginning of the 20th century but is currently taken very seriously by researchers from the most diverse scientific disciplines, from Biology to Theoretical Physics: it is about synchronicity.

And, since I have brought it up, I find it impossible to resist the temptation to tell a personal anecdote related to it.

One of my best friends owns a family mansion from the seventeenth century in a semi-abandoned village in the plains of Lleida, specifically in the County of Urgell, in a territory dedicated to the cultivation of cereal. It is dry, very cold in winter and hot in summer. The number of inhabitants of the little town, made up of a church and three short streets overlooking a practically impassable local road, does not exceed two or three inhabitants in the off season. Just a dozen in the peak season. During the day you can only hear the shrill of cicadas, you can gaze at the horizon for hours without a single human figure interfering with your vision, and the sunsets would fill Romain Rolland with an oceanic feeling. The mansion, somewhat dilapidated, with three floors plus a basement, wooden beams and thick stone walls, has great charm. An ideal place to isolate yourself from the world and enjoy moments of introspection, native foods accompanied by succulent red wine and uplifting conversations about being and nothingness by the fireplace when low temperatures take over outside.

In the scorching summer of 2002 both the house, in which we rebuilt the decoration of Thelema Abbey, and its vast surroundings, so "Sicilian", served as a set for the film *Perdurabo* (Where is Aleister Crowley).[31] On almost every occasion that I have visited the place, whether for recreational or professional purposes, I have witnessed phenomena that we could classify as curious, if not extraordinary. Perdurabo's own filming was no exception. But the most astonishing case, in my opinion, was the one that I am going to relate now.

It was the fall of 2001. I remember that it was Sunday and that the weather was running listless around noon. My friend and I had sat on the low wall that surrounds the tiny churchyard of the little town. We were immersed in one of our usual talks about mysteries and parallel realities. A mere

---

31. TIMÓN, M. (producer) and ATANES, C. (director). (2003). *Perdurabo (Where is Aleister Crowley?)*. Spain: FortKnox Audiovisual.

two dozen meters separated us from the road, beyond which stretched the endless plain of wheat fields. If throughout a whole day, more than two cars and a fruit truck made a fleeting appearance on that road, we considered it a traffic jam. The solitude that surrounded us was thus almost absolute.

Inspired by the proximity of the cemetery, I began to explain to my friend something that I had recently discovered in some Internet unknown corner and that I have not found since then. It was the chronicle of an experiment carried out by two Australians, a father and his son. The experiment was based on a fairly reasonable assumption: it follows from the possibility of time travel that, if one day it is achieved, the future chrononauts would be in a position to visit our present, that is, their past. Unfortunately, the apparent absence of chrononauts from the future in our time suggests that time travel will continue to be an unattainable milestone. In any case, that we do not see them does not mean that they are not there, however incomprehensible it may be that someone could be interested in visiting a century as disappointing as ours in every way. They may have a reserved nature and prefer not to meddle in our affairs ostensibly. In fact, it would be the most plausible, given the danger of going around unleashing temporal paradoxes.

In short, the fact is that the Australian father and son, intrigued by this matter, resolved to clear up their doubts by getting down to work. They wrote a note placing the chrononauts at a precise time, day and place, something like: "If you have the ability to go back in time, manifest on such a day at such o'clock in such a place." The site in question was a well indicated location within the cemetery of an Australian city, surely Sydney, but I dare not say so. They put the note in a time capsule, headed for the graveyard, dug a hole in the ground, buried the capsule, and sat down to wait.

When the clock indicated the exact time, nothing worthy of a Marvel blockbuster happened. There was no lightning and no wormholes opened in the air. But, at that precise moment, a black limousine stopped at the top of a nearby hill. He stood motionless for a few seconds, as if the occupants were watching them, and then it was gone. It's not a particularly portentous event, let's face it. That's the truth. It is a rather modest event in a big city cemetery, where black cars must frequently go. Which did not stop the investigating couple from feeling an unsettling sensation.

And at that point in the story I was when my friend looked down the road. A car had stopped in front of us. A black limousine with tinted windows. On that dusty road, where one can tend to read the complete works of Marcel Proust without fear of being run over, in that country of cicadas in the middle of nowhere where no one would think of going to stop by mistake, a luxurious black limousine had stopped in front of us just as I was talking about another black limousine stopped in another cemetery on the antipodes of the world. It remained motionless for a few seconds, as if the occupants were observing us, and it resumed his march towards nowhere. My friend and I looked at each other in silence. I still remember the expression on his face. He must still remember mine.

I do not want to sin of vanity, but it must be admitted that Carl Gustav Jung's famous encounter with synchronicity pales next to the episode I have just related. I will remind the forgetful that Jung was listening to a patient who was telling him how in a dream she received a golden beetle as a gift when the psychiatrist heard a blow behind him: a beetle of the Cetonia aurata type had just been slammed against the glass of the window when wanting to enter the room.

There are three ways of dealing with a coincidence of this type, and I already anticipate that two are doomed to failure beforehand: we can appeal to causality, chance or synchronicity:

The explanation based on causality collapses immediately because neither science nor logic can in any way explain the material or energetic mechanism by which the mind of my friend, Jung, his patient or mine can redirect the trajectory of cars and beetles when her unconscious or mine requires them. There is no wave or particle to explain that. Causation plays no role here.

As in the Three Little Pigs tale, please, no one is offended by the simile, here there are no personal allusions; they could be rabbits or lambs, but the tale is as it is, when the wolf, blowing and blowing, knocks down the house of causality, its occupant has the habit of fleeing in terror and running to take refuge in the house of chance. The house of no matter what. But the probability that a golden beetle will come when it is mentioned, and let alone the probability that a black limousine appears and stops in a deserted place, in front of a cemetery, just at the moment when we allude to another black limousine that emerged and he stopped at another cemetery, bordering on the ridiculous in that case and the paltry in this one, emptying of meaning the very concept of chance. If chance is this, the dictionary definition will have to be reconsidered.

In the tale, after the second catastrophe, the little pigs run to hide in the third house. On the contrary, in real life, many people prefer to stay and parley with the wolf in an unsuccessful attempt to persuade him that he is hallucinating and that the house, as much as a mass of rubble, is still standing. However, as much as they insist on not being aware of it, it turns out that there is a third little pig, the oldest, who has built a third house, the safest. Young piglets, less boastful than some humans, rush to her. It is the house of synchronicity.

Carl Gustav Jung elaborated the concept of synchronicity as a result of the beetle incident, and it can be summarized in the acausal and significant coincidence in time of two events, one psychic and the other external, objective. In Jung's definition we find a manifest link between mind and matter. And it expressly underlines the acausal nature of the phenomenon. At no time does he claim that the mind causes a change in the disposition of matter. What causes synchronicity is a third element, an underlying, hidden articulation, which functions outside the deterministic cause-effect laws of classical physics and which reveals the essentially organic, interrelated, holistic character of nature. A dynamic that transcends mind and matter but at the same time sustains them.

The physicist F. David Peat calls this implied, generative and formative order "objective intelligence", which unfolds in the infinite variety of relationships and events in our universe and constitutes an explanation of phenomena, structures and behaviors, Peat cites dissipative structures from Prigogine, the collective nature of slime mold and electron gas,[32] in which matter deviates from the iron-clad mechanistic path of causality and seems to become self-aware.

This informational field of universal extension not only does not enter into contradiction but also protects and sheds a new light on the heterogeneous assortment of ideas. Phenomena that have precipitated like coffee grounds in the pot of chaos magic: morphic resonances, the semiotic web, the chaos-etheric paradigm, the influence of the observer on the observed, the holistic nature of the universe, the higher dimensions ... Pieces of a puzzle that, once fitted into each other. They show an image that I would dare to describe like this: a universe holistic, in which our four-dimensional space-time and its quantum indeterminacy and chaotic acausality are the projection of an order or "objective intelligence". Encompassing ours but also extending through one or more higher dimensions, constituting a semiotic network of pure information in interaction, resonance and

---

32. *Vid* PEAT, F. D. (1988).

constant feedback with our mind and with the matter that constitutes and surrounds us. [33]

We are no longer talking, returning to magical praxis, of determining the state of imperceptible elements of the subatomic world, but of increasing and enhancing the bidirectional, generative and formative flow that connects our mind with that "objective intelligence" and through it, with our objective and subjective reality, so intimately interrelated that even the conspicuous mathematician and cosmologist Roger Penrose advocates a new formulation of physics to understand consciousness. [34]

If our collective unconscious archetypes, the synchronicities occurrence and the ability to achieve by non-physical means the knowledge or perception of what

---

33. "You may scoff, but in 2003 the philosopher Nick Bostrom of Oxford University published a paper laying out reasons to think that we are pretty likely to be living in a simulation. And the simulation hypothesis has gained influential supporters. Neil deGrasse Tyson, director of the Hayden Planetarium and America's de facto astronomer laureate, finds it plausible. The visionary tech entrepreneur Elon Musk says there's almost no chance that we're living in "base reality." The New Yorker reported earlier this year that "two tech billionaires" — it didn't say whether Musk is one of them — "have gone so far as to secretly engage scientists to work on breaking us out of the simulation." *The New York Times*. Recovered from: https://www.nytimes.com/2016/12/12/opinion/can-evolution-have-a-higher-purpose.html

34. "I have the feeling that the new theory that unifies the Physics of the very large with that of the very small will have a lot to say on the subject of consciousness. We need a new formulation of Physics to understand it." SABADELL, M. A. (February 2000). [Interview with Roger Penrose] *MUY Interesante*, 225.

happens in remote places, for example, if all this I say, is explained in terms of taking contact with something similar to a morphic field, then nothing seems to prevent us from generating consequences by shaking or pulsing that field. Quite the contrary: everything seems to indicate that it is in our power to do so.

Although it is inevitable that at this point a doubt assails us: if that informational field unfolds in a higher spatial dimension, how can we exert any influence on it from our three-dimensional confinement, Well, let's go by steps.

In the first place, this alleged confinement is no more than a conjecture. That something is invisible does not mean that it does not exist, like chrononauts. It may sound like a truism, but it is convenient to insist on it from time to time. A shark is unable to see its own dorsal fin and it still remains an essential part of its anatomy and plays an essential role in its mobility and, by extension, in its survival. Let us pay attention to what, following a logical line of reasoning, Rudolf Steiner deduced:

> "If we draw the correct conclusions, we must say that just as a one-dimensional being can perceive only points, a two-dimensional being only one dimension, and a three-dimensional being only two dimensions, a being that perceives three dimensions must be a four-dimensional being. Because we can delineate external beings in three dimensions and manipulate three-dimensional spaces, we must be fourth-dimensional beings. Just as a cube can perceive only two dimensions and not its own third

dimension, it is also true that we human beings cannot perceive the fourth dimension in which we live."[35]

Second, sensory inaccessibility to hyperdimensional spaces does not preclude an indirect approach that facilitates cognitive apprehension. Physicists and mathematicians alike have long been used to working in n-dimensional spaces. M-theory, for example, which is a unification theory of the five superstring theories, tells us about compactions of six, seven and even eleven dimensions in subatomic spaces.

Third, we can also challenge sensory inaccessibility. Art has provided us with very palpable projections of geometries imbued with strange dimensionalities, examples are innumerable, ranging from the engravings of M. C. Escher to the animated recreations of auto-recursive fractal complexities and rotating tesseracts that we can contemplate in countless Internet videos; recreations that produce a very forceful feeling of reality or, at least, of verisimilitude. But the perceptual exploration of hyperdimensionality has gone further. There are those who are not content with mere projections. Charles Howard Hinton, the fourth-dimensional visionary who invented the term tesseract, claimed to have seen four-dimensional objects. To achieve this he used an ingenious method that he disclosed in 1888, in his book *A New Era of Thought*,[36] a compendium of mathematical speculations tinged with his peculiar mysticism. Referring

---

35. STEINER, R. (2016: 17)

36. HINTON, C. H., STOTT, A. B., FALK, H. J. (2015)

to the two-dimensional retina, which is what allows us to visualize three-dimensional objects, he invented a three-dimensional retina to visualize four-dimensional objects. This retina was not a physical device, but a mental one, although it had previously relied on a physical device for training: a set of twenty-seven, sixty-four or one hundred and twenty-five colored cubes whose relative arrangement inside a larger cube had to be memorized. To that end, Hinton had assigned Latin names to each line, side, and vertex of the cubes. The plan was for each of these small cubes to function like the imaginary ommatidium of a fly's eye, or a photoelectric cell of a camera's CCD device, but not placed on a two-dimensional surface but rather in a three-dimensional structure that would allow us to contemplate tesseracts with the eyes of imagination. Not the shadow of a tesseract, but the direct, albeit mental, perception of the tesseract.

Regardless of the fact that, as Hinton and Steiner suspected, we are four-dimensional beings living in a four-dimensional space despite our senses not being aware of it, and regardless of the fact that, perhaps, perceptual access to that four-dimensionality is not so forbidden as it might seem, there is something else to add to the viability of an interaction with a hyperdimensional informational field: precisely, that it is an interaction. A two-way street.

Even if our body was completely embedded in the three-dimensional coordinates, our mind is not, since it is not spatially limited. It is able to conceive and envision hyperdimensional spaces and is a recipient of informational resonances that come from the influence of matter and the mind in the informational web. That is to say, the mind is both a receiver and a transmitter, because it is part of that network in as intrinsic a way as waves are part of a mass of oceanic water.

I do not know the specific mechanism by which the interaction occurs, but it does not escape me to a greater or lesser extent than the specific mechanism that allows the mind to interact with the body. Ultimately, it is not because it is assumed and routine that it is truly marvelous that our will decides to move a finger and that the finger moves. It is difficult now to resolve the old debate that Descartes started about how the res cogitans can affect the extensive res, which so many philosophers have since dealt with. Carroll settles the issue in his *Liber Kaos*, where he formulates his CMT (Chaos Magic Theory), a kind of synthesis of the previously exposed paradigms, in which he takes sides with materialism and assigns to the mental events the quality of material structures, thus erasing at a stroke the problem of their interaction with the network of informational fields, which he prefers to call etheric patterns.

Moreover, according to Carroll's CMT, and thanks to its doubling of the temporal dimension in pseudo time and shadow time,[37] there is no asymmetry between the mechanism of reception and emission, sometimes making blurred the distinction between spell, pattern emission, mind

---

37. CARROLL, P.J. (1992: 29)

to ether, and divination, pattern reception, ether to mind[38].
Fortunately, it is not necessary to choose urgently between materialistic monism or idealistic dualism, because the elucidation of the most impenetrable philosophical questions is not an immediate requirement, or even a necessary one, for the practice of magic.

It is in this area, that of practice, not that of theory, where the often-alluded meta-paradigm intervenes, the exposition of which I have insisted on delaying. The meta-paradigm is not a world view. It is a way of working, a utilitarian relationship, an ephemeral use of paradigms. It is the most disruptive contribution, I said, of the chaos magic. Its most distinctive way of proceeding.

But let's undo a mistake: as I showed in the diagram, the meta-paradigm does not encompass all paradigms, it only establishes a pragmatic relationship between them. There is a hierarchy: a main paradigm, the informational one, connected but not contained in the meta-paradigm, which is nourished by the others. Chaos magic does not consist in the eclectic use of all paradigms, but rather, as Carroll's own inventory of six models shows, it is firmly rooted in the informational paradigm and reveals itself eclectic only when, at its convenience, it uses other paradigms.

More specifically, from one: the psychological. Because

---

38. CARROLL, P. J. (1992: 23-24)

the psychological paradigm is, in itself, another meta-paradigm, since it uses the paradigms that precede it at will, knowing that they are useful but not necessarily true. Chaos magic, whilst using the psychological one also uses the rest, shares with the psychological one the conviction that, to work, the consciousness is sufficient with the elements it conceives, regardless of the objective existence of those elements.

In this way, to access the informational field and make a query in the Akashic Records, it is convenient to invoke our Holy Guardian Angel. He is invoked, even if, as good skeptics, we do not believe in the existence of holy guardian angels. This is the meta-paradigm: to resort, by means of the suspension of our disbelief in a premeditated and provisional way, to any inspiring model contained in our toolbox, whether it is a previous magical system, such as Wicca or Golden Dawn ceremonial magic, from a mythology drawn from fantasy literature, like Oz or Cthulhu Mythos, or from a fictional pop culture universe, like Dr. Strange comics or Hellraiser saga. Or something from our own harvest. Or, as already put, from a combination of this with that. The only thing that matters is that we fiddle around in the wardrobe of magic, culture and our imagination and from their chests we extract the bowler, Russian, peakless, straw, porkpie, top hat, cap or diving helmet which most profitably contributes to our autosuggestion. With such carelessness and utilitarianism a chaoist leads. In fact, the founders of chaos magic have on different occasions expressed their rejection of any kind of metaphysical conception of magic. And to avoid all metaphysical solemnity and avoid the dangerous seduction of siren songs, what is recommended is a joyful and varied eclecticism, a go sucking from flower to flower that does not commit itself to a single model for a single second beyond the strictly indispensable time. And do not miss the laughter.

Of course, this lighthearted eclecticism is controversial. As mentioned before, chaoism has been accused of being utilitarian and immoral by magicians attached to other currents for example neo-pagan. Some chaoists, like Ellwood, have responded to these accusations with greater or lesser success.[39] But apart from the fact that eclecticism and its implementation do not necessarily have to be disrespectful, the truth is that it is easy to hurt susceptibilities. No believer, especially if he is a devotee, likes any intruder to fondle his iconography or the higher entities in which he places his faith, without having first washing his hands. And the greater the apparent lightness with which it is made, the greater the potential offense. The Navajo people represent a blatant case: they chain one claim after another, powerless in the face of the indiscriminate appropriation in the West of their aesthetic and ceremonial elements, often under the guise of a sense of "homage", but all too often with a purpose merely pecuniary or on a pseudo-mystical whim, and always from an inexcusable ignorance of the spiritual and sacred depth of what is being misrepresented.

Respect for beliefs is a much more complex and delicate

---

39. ELLWOOD, T. (2008: 95)

issue than it might seem at first glance. So much so that blasphemy, derision or offense to religious feelings is a crime included in the penal code of at least one out of every four countries in the world. Regardless of the discussion about whether lack of respect should be a crime or not, or when a feeling is religious, do we really have to respect beliefs, dogmas and rites. Should the faith be shielded from the attacks of freedom of expression or other cults? In this respect, the debate on the right to offense competes in pertinacity with that of the *res cogitans* and the res extensa.

I myself, who for a long time have thought, and to a large extent still think, that respect should not be devoted to beliefs but to people, and their freedom of thought. I have ended up harboring certain doubts about the extent to which we respect people, if in that respect we do not include their beliefs to some extent. And I confess that, according to my congenital intellectual hesitancy and the little respect with which I try to put my own convictions in permanent jeopardy, I have not reached as irrevocable a conclusion as I would like. The line that separates offense to feelings, and incitement to hatred, is not always evident. History shows us that it is not uncommon for the outrage of individuals and groups to be accompanied, if not preceded, by contempt for their beliefs. Outrage instigated ordinarily by beliefs that are themselves very little respectable. All right, we can accept that it is not the same to respect a person's right to have a belief than to respect that particular belief. But in practice, the nuance tends to fade – I cannot respect the right of an indigenous community to be animist and at the same time blatantly usurp its sacred elements and denature them without incurring a certain cynicism. Doing so requires the deployment of a double standard, perhaps innocuous for some, but which is a bit embarrassing for me.

Although deviating so much from the subject may cause us to lose sight of a substantial aspect: a fashion show is one thing and a chaoist ritual is another. The first is held in public view, the second behind closed doors. The offense largely vanishes when there is no offended. That is, if there is, it will no longer be an offended believer but, a disgusted preternatural entity. Here it is equally appropriate to advise caution. Part of the risks assumed by a magician is the possibility of running into unknown forces, believe them or not, and of inciting their hostility, be it because of his clumsiness, foolishness or irreverence. And it must be emphasized that a chaoist magician always believes, even for a limited time. That is the meta-paradigm. If he did not accept as true the belief in which he has chosen to believe in a certain moment, we would not be talking about a meta-paradigm, but about something else.

It is clear that this belief is based on a somewhat artificial suspension of disbelief, allow me the pleonasm. But the game has unsuspected depths. Sometimes you start by believing a little and you end up creating. For example, remember the Indian cemetery sequence from *Jeremiah Johnson*.[40] In order to rescue settlers isolated by snow, the

---

40. WIZAN, J. (producer) and POLLACK, S. (director). (1972). *Jeremiah Johnson*. U.S.A.: Warner Bros.

army requires the services of Jeremiah, a lone trapper who knows the mountains well. The character, played by Robert Redford, is reluctant to lead the column of soldiers through a Crow graveyard, but eventually gives in to the urging of the commanding officer. The incursion into sacred land has dire consequences that I am not going to relate so as not to gut the film to those who have not seen it yet. The events are exposed in an interesting way: it is understood that the Crow Indians take revenge for the desecration, but this understanding results only from the order in which the events occur, since we are never shown any Crow witnessing said desecration. This is an intentional and, of course, very suggestive omission, it leaves us wondering who was offended, the Crow who are alive or the Crow who are buried in the cemetery. Ultimately, the important thing is that there has been a consequence and that Jeremiah Johnson, an unbeliever at first, but a believer at the end of the day, feared there would be. And he has triggered it. There is some self-fulfilling prophecy there. That is, of creation.

When it comes to fingering it, the meta-paradigm is equivalent to buying many tickets in a lottery: if there is a chance, chaoist eclecticism exponentially increases the chances of touching where it hurts. But without risk there is no glory and, it must also be said, whoever is free from sin cast the first stone: the accusations leveled against chaoism can quickly turn against the culprits, in terms of beliefs and ceremonies, be they magical or religious, as in art, science and all cultural manifestations in general, we will hardly find a case of Adamic originality. On the contrary, what we will easily find, wherever we put the focus, will be the most recent layer of a succession of heresies superimposed one on top of the other, born of an endless series of splits, syncretisms and apostasies whose origin is diluted in the mists of prehistory.

Of course, it is convenient to leave an issue settled once and for all. I have alluded to eclecticism, not nihilism. Chaos magic relativizes in a restricted way, that is, depending on the utility that it can extract from it. Its eclectic utilitarianism does not amount to extreme relativism, as someone could erroneously interpret it. There is no more nihilism or moral relativism in chaos magic, than that suggested, in a personal capacity, by those who profess it. Chaos magic is not a transposition to the magical terrain of individualist anarchism. Some of its most famous champions, and presumably a large percentage of sympathizers (in which even I include myself on odd days), seem to identify with that ideology. It is absurd to accuse chaos magic of moral relativism, for not adhering to any traditional faith. In the same way, as it would be to pretend that an agnostic, by the mere fact of being an agnostic, has a lack of ethical principles, that prevent him from distinguishing good from evil.

But if moral relativism is not intrinsic to chaos magic, even less so is epistemological relativism. In an irrefutable way and in my opinion, and without denying but not affirming the existence of spirits or subtle energies, that is, without discussing their existence, the magic of chaos is based on fundamental beliefs. Beliefs that it does not question, those that make up the Great Paradigm. But even when it didn't, in the most extreme case, there would still be a core belief, that chaos magic could never set aside, purely tautological: the belief that, no matter how or why, magic works.

That said, the recommendation to jump from one belief to another, beliefs of a secondary order, emanating from the Great Paradigm, is pertinent. Since it is not advisable to hold one single belief for too long, lingering between the cozy sheets of the famous comfort zone, an accommodation that sooner or later will cause a decrease in the magician's creative powers. Which must be as much or more dangerous, a slide down the slope of obsessive disorders. There should be no more ties in the magical task than those that link the will with the goals that the magician has proposed to achieve. And no better training than the permanent revision of the principles, thesis and tastes.

In order to reorganize the mind to discover our True Will, Crowley invites us to always disagree in conversations and Carroll to substitute our everyday habits[41] with the aim of producing "inspiration and enlightenment through disordering our belief structures. Humor, random belief, counter-information, and misinformation are its techniques."[42] Very helpful advice, in my opinion, even apart from its use with strictly magical intentions.

It is truly disheartening to look around and see how

---

41. CARROLL, P.J. (1987: 18)
42. CARROLL, P.J. (1987: 115)

chained we are to our own prejudices. We live under the rule of confirmation bias. We have erected a throne for opinion and taste, this is not the place to analyze the plethora of causes that have led to it, although, obviously, the least relevant is not the ease of diffusion that new technologies have made available to us, under whose aegis we build authentic armor of closure and fanaticism.

Also note the interrelation between affinities of supposedly unconnected spheres, ranging from the aesthetic to the ideological. From the haircut to hatred to a certain political options, refractory to any reasoning. Deaf to any evidence: if A, then B; if I am against C, then in all probability I am also against D and in favor of E and F. They are "thought packages", which points to their extrinsic character. Inadvertently extrinsic but assumed as our own, inborn, deeply us, since what could be more us than our taste. The Praetorian guard of our conscious mind is quick to alert us. In short, it is in that thick burial mound, only apparently coherent, of contradictions, presumptions, habits and beliefs that bury our True Will. The magical tradition invites us to dig, in order to acquire the ability, in Crowley's words, to coordinate our mental muscles to make a movement with intention. And incidentally, in my words, to show to our taste and who is boss here.

A good chaoist must inflexibly regard imaginative means as mere boulders on which to rest his feet to traverse the one-way current, provisional tools whose usefulness will be exhausted in their inescapable condition of ballast. He must also program its obsolescence. And replace them without bitterness, when they are still at the peak of their fruitfulness. The constant search for new imaginative territories is, in itself, a spur for creativity and cannot be unrewarded.

Take, for example, one who has built his conceptual building on *Star Wars* and one day decides, contrite, to cut to the chase. The love that *Star Wars* fans feel for this fictional universe is well known to all, and it is easy to imagine the pain associated with its eventual abandonment. But such a sacrifice will be, as I said, highly rewarded when, after closing that door, another one opens that will lead him, for example, to *Star Trek*, a world without a doubt more substantial and stimulating that will not force him to swallow with such embarrassing occurrences as Jar Jar Binks or midi-chlorians. Anyone gifted with criteria would qualify this relief as a clear qualitative advance. However, this new station cannot be the last of the journey either. There is no last station and the advance must always continue.

Also, sometimes unforeseen circumstances can speed up the move. For example, having chosen the *Star Trek: The Original Series* saga, the newcomer may soon see their enthusiasm darkened by an eerie sense of a funeral that does not have a positive impact on their work. To this day, at the time of writing these lines, only four of the seven actors who played the crew members of the USS Enterprise NCC-1701 are still alive. And that the four that remain are already octogenarians does not contribute, in principle, to overly relying on a very long survival, I hope I am wrong and God bless them with an immeasurably long and prosperous existence.

Strictly speaking, contingencies on the real reverse of a fictional world should not be relevant to the magician's purposes. Authors and actors die; characters, plots and settings remain. But it is possible, especially in the case of audiovisual media, that the identification of one with the other is, in singularly iconic cases, so inextricable and difficult to dissociate, that the effort it will take to avoid their influence is not worth it. If the impression of being a practicing necromancer infuriates our apprehension, to the point of disrupting our attention and hindering our work, we immediately shelve and set out to fish in more profitable waters. Whether they are the product of other people's minds, or, preferably, our own or, also the magic of chaos is an *all-you-can-eat buffet*, a mix of one and the other. As Hawkins points out, "what is important for the Chaos Magician of today, is to interpret his/her own magic in his/her own way. We can learn a lot from others, but ultimately the magic must come from oneself."[43] There are no more rules or limits here than self-imposed ones.

Thus, for example, the meta-paradigm enables the practice within the chaoist framework of ceremonial magic in the old fashioned way. In a spatially limited space, located outside of the consensual reality, what Phil Hine calls the Free Zone, obviously related to his contemporary Hakim Bey's TAZ, or Temporary Autonomous Zone. A space traditionally called a temple, resorting to a series of tools previously transfigured from common objects to magic objects, such as the dagger, the wand, the sword, the

---

43. HAWKINS, J. D. (1996: 111)

irreplaceable incense,[44] etc. And organized around the invocation or evocation of entities in order to generate changes in reality according to our Will.

Chaoism favors the practice of a free-form ritual but does not exclude rigorous practice, provisionally adjusted to dogma and tradition. Unlike the days when Crowley wrote and published his *Magick in Theory and Practice*, today it is not difficult to find grimoires, forms, Golden Dawn secret documents [sic] and correspondence tables in all kinds of bookstores, libraries and, of course, the Internet.

I recommend to those interested in scrutinizing the principles of this modality, that they begin by going to what is still the table of correspondences par excellence today, the *Liber 777 Vel Prolegomena Symbolica Ad Systemam Sceptico-Mysticae Viae Explicande, Fundamentum Hieroglyphicum Sanctissimorum Scientiae Summae*[45], also, of course, by Aleister Crowley. The author, through an overwhelming array of indexes, boxes and tabulated lists, establishes equivalences between the mystical numbers of the Sephiroth and the Heavens of Assiah, the four elements, the Olympic Planetary Spirits, diseases, the Paths of the Sepher Yetzirah, Tarot Trumps, Hexagram correspondences, Egyptian Gods, Alchemy metals, Hindu Deities, Apostles, Magical Weapons, the Mansions of the Moon, imaginary animals, body parts,

---

44. "We can think of the incense smoke as a medium which provides both smell, and a material for forming an appearance." ELLWOOD, T. (2008: 112)

45. CROWLEY, A. (2004)

the Four Noble Truths, precious stones, perfumes and sandals, the Ten Earths in Seven Palaces, vegetable and mineral drugs, the Coptic alphabet, Choirs of Angels in Briah, Goetic Demons, Geomantic Intelligences and the Ten Divisions of the Body of God. There is more, but I don't pretend to be exhaustive either.

For those who, subjected to the rattling and narrowness of urban life and do not have time or room in their apartment to get involved in these tasks, the meta-paradigm offers countless more affordable alternatives, such as the establishment of an astral temple, I will return to it. The elaboration of a personal correspondence table, adapted to their needs and purposes,[46] and a *modus operandi* exquisite in its simplicity and efficiency, the technique most appreciated by chaoists, the core technique, one might say, of chaos magic: sigilization, Austin Osman Spare's greatest contribution to 20th and 21st century magic.

Spare, artist and magician, friend for a couple of years and companion of Crowley in the initiatic societies Golden Dawn and Astrum Argentum, later distanced himself from him by doctrinal discrepancies and incompatibility of temperaments. Which should not surprise us in the case of the abrasive Crowley. Spare built his own magical system, called Zos Kia, and completely reworked the sigilization system.

Spare did not invent sigils, but he made renewed use of them that made them the practical core of chaos magic

---

46. As recommended in DUNN, P. (2005: 10)

decades later. In *The Book of Pleasure*, Spare defines sigils as "monograms of thought, for the Government of energy".[47]

> "Whatever you really want, you can get. The want first rises in the conscious mind, but you have to make the subconscious desire it too. And you can do this by inventing a symbol of the thing you want, wealth, a woman, fame or a country cottage, it's all alike. The symbol drops down into the subconscious. You have to forget all about it. In fact, you must play hide-and-seek with yourself. And while you're wanting that particular thing or person, you must resolutely starve all your lesser desires. By doing that, you make the whole self, conscious and subconscious, flow toward your main object. And you'll obtain it."[48]

Spare is credited with achieving several wonders in the presence of witnesses, such as altering the weather or the sudden materialization of objects. I cannot confirm or deny such assumptions since I was not present, but what is clear is that Spare took his magical work very seriously.

Making a sigil is a simple task. The literature on the subject abounds and the Internet is full of explanations, handbooks, cookbooks and tips, so I will not go into the details. There are different types of sigil, based on the voice, mantras, or on automatic drawing, but the most common

---

47. RASULA, J. And MCCAFFERY, S. (1998: 369)
48. Austin Osman Spare quoted in SEMPLE, G. (1995: 30)

by far is the graphic type. It basically consists of writing a wish in capital letters, in the most concrete and synthetic way possible, for example, "I WANT TO KNOW RITA",, crossing out the repeated letters so that none appear more than once and, with the ones that remain, "IWANTOMER",, compose an emblem where the initial text is unrecognizable.

It is an entertaining activity, which is worth doing with care so that the result is endowed with a certain elegance or, at least, conciseness. The ideogram can be repeated as many times as necessary, repositioning, stretching or deleting what we consider necessary until we achieve something that

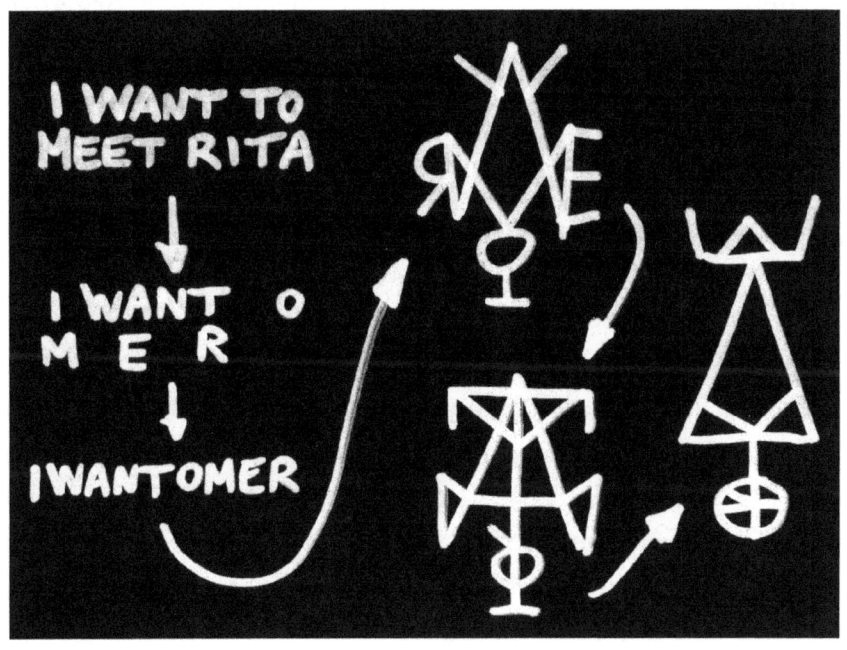

Fig. 03

satisfies the expectations of our aesthetic sensibility. The physical support of the sigil can be any surface that allows writing: a paper, a blackboard, a parchment, a (thick) carrot puree, a mass of clay, a computer screen, a glass covered in mist ...

The illustration above shows the transformation of "I WANT TO MEET RITA" statement into a sigil. The impossibility, from the ignorance of the message that originated it, of inferring the implicit meaning of the resulting hieroglyph becomes evident. The wisest thing a discerning observer could describe would be something like the dance of a girl perched on a unicycle.

It is advisable not to be too quick to write the opening sentence. Ideally, it should produce the most performative sigil possible. Therefore, it is better not to write the first thing that comes to mind and take our time to find the most convenient formulation. For example, "I WANT TO MEET RITA" would be the mere statement of a wish. Desire is taken for granted, as is courage to the soldier, and simply stating it leads to no result.

Not all chaoists agree with me on this point, but I personally consider it important to keep in mind that desire and will are different things, and that magic consists in generating changes according to will, not desire. "MY WILL IS TO MEET RITA", for example. Or "I WANT TO MEET RITA", the phrase I used as an example. It is a little better, because it denotes conscious will, the assumption of actually wanting to fulfill a wish. But it is not the best by far. A more restrictive version, closer to a strong conviction in the success of the operation, of the type "I AM GOING TO MEET RITA", would be preferable. Thus the fulfillment of the wish would be taken for granted. The will must be accompanied by determination and confidence. On the other hand, I consider that it is not advisable to venture further. Using an authoritarian tone, such as "RITA, LET ME KNOW YOU" can cause a collision between opposing wills and spoil the effect. Eventually, it is highly probable that Rita also has a will of her own, and she does not have to obey, what's more, the normal and desirable thing would be for her not to obey, the orders of a total stranger. Actually, self-directed sigils, intended to carry out an action are less problematic and much more effective than those directed at third parties.

As I have already pointed out, the "word" derived from the opening sentence, can also be transformed into a sound sigil if we choose to declaim it as a mantra. For example, from "I WANT TO KNOW RITA" is derived "IWANTOMER", which in turn can be rearranged as "TIWORAMEN", "MONRAWETI", "TEMAWINOR" and the successive list of squeakings that may result from other combinations. In case of opting for sound sigilization, we will choose a word that is suggestive to the ear and that avoids the unnecessary rush of dying choking on our own tongue.

A visual sigil has the advantage of discretion. We can sigilize on a paper napkin in a coffee shop or on an entrance ticket to the opera while we attend an enactment of The Magic Flute without anyone noticing what we are doing.

But if discretion is not a priority, sound sigil also has its advantages: if we chant aloud "MONRAWETI" or "IWANTOMER" as we walk through public spaces, it is most likely that we will not have to wait in line at any teller machine. Actors who repeat their text aloud to memorize it, also find it easy to find empty seats around them on the bus. Speaking alone on the street, is like walking inside a transparent plastic ball that is pushing people away as we go along. Which, all things considered, is an eminently magical achievement. In any case, nothing prevents us from combining the sound with the visual expression of the sigil, if we like, which will result in greater synergy at the time of activation or, as they say in magic jargon, at the time of charging the stealth.

Morrison claims that "sigils always work", with a delay in effectiveness, in his case, of three days, three weeks, or three months[49]. He refers, I understand, to well-crafted and well-charged sigils. In other words, sigilization always works, as long as it's done right. Acquiring skill in this art, as in all arts, requires practice. I have no doubt that Mr. Morrison has gained a great mastery of the matter.

It should be noted, however, that it is not inherently antimagic to lend an extra hand to sigil when the opportunity presents itself. For example, if we want to meet Miss Rita and we find out that she is invited to the party that some mutual friends will celebrate tonight, the smartest thing is that we try to go too. With the sigil in place, our appearance

---

49. Morrison, G. "Pop magic!". Metzger, Richard (2014: 18)

and a bit of luck, it is even possible that they introduce her to us. If, on the contrary, we disdain the occasion that is given us and choose to stay at home rereading Fulcanelli's *Le Mystère des Cathédrales*, trusting that the morphic resonances will do all the work for us, we will be feeding the risk of shrinking the probability of success.

What I just said may sound like a joke, but it isn't. Magic does not produce miracles, only effects likely to appear so. Crowley was very clear when he stated that you "cannot produce a thunderstorm unless the materials exist in the air at the time, and a Magician who could make rain in Cumberland might fail lamentably in the Sahara."[50] The universe has its rules, its inertia, reality is tremendously stubborn and foolish to pretend otherwise.

So we have a carefully crafted sigil in our hands. For it to work you have to charge it. What is charging a sigil, It consists of sending it. In the same way that the ancient Romans threw their defixiones written on lead sheets into a well or buried them underground so that the gods could read and execute them,[51] the sigil must be uploaded to the informational network, exactly like how we upload a video

---

50. CROWLEY A. (1994: 101) Annotation in which the euphoria of the following fragment, extracted from *Book 4*, must be subsumed: «It is only necessary to believe that a thing must be to bring it about. This belief must not be an emotional or an intellectual one. It resides in a deeper portion of the mind, yet a portion not so deep but that most men, probably all successful men, will understand these words, having experience of their own with which they can compare it.» (*Book 4*, Part I, Chapter VI: Dhyana)

51. DUNN, P. (2005: 107)

to Youtube after producing it. This is achieved, as Spare explains, by making it descend into the unconscious by playing hide and seek with ourselves, do not be unnecessarily obsessed with the apparent up/down contradiction; both uploading and descending play a rhetorical role here. The steps to take are: reach a state of gnosis, inject the sigil into the unconscious and then forget it.

Basically, there are two paths that lead to the state of gnosis, although Phil Hine adds a third, Indifferent Vacuity, that of no-mind, Non-Disinterest,[52] and they consist in provoking oneself a great excitement or a great inhibition or serenity: orgasm, anger, panic, drunkenness, drugs, meditation, extreme fatigue[53]... At the peak of abandonment of consciousness is when you have to visualize the sigil. A method, in short, analogous to that used in ceremonial magic to produce a dramatic climax: "At the moment when the excitement becomes ungovernable, when the whole conscious being of the Magician undergoes a spiritual spasm, at that moment must he utter the supreme adjuration."[54] Once the charge is consummated, the physical sigil must be destroyed, burned, erased, undone, buried..., and its mental assimilation forgotten. Very important: forgotten. I insist: forgotten.

---

52. Hine, P. (2009: 41)

53. The methods are innumerable. Ellwood, T. (2008: 86) explains how to charge a sigil with a video game.

54. Crowley A. (1994: 116-117)

Any conscious reminiscence of the sigil or the desire that inspired it will now represent an undesirable interference in the development of its task. "Directly we desire, we have lost all; 'we are' what we desire, therefore we never obtain. Desire nothing, and there is nothing that you shall not realize."[55] Although there are few who assure, Grant Morrison[56] among them, that the destruction of stealth is not essential, Taylor Ellwood, for example, paints them and hangs them on the walls, well in sight[57], or that, for the sake of greater impetus it is even convenient to charge it more than once. There is no obstacle to this, I suppose, as long as oblivion acts and that subsequent recharges are carried out after the time necessary to guarantee the unintelligibility of the sigil. That is, we no longer know what exactly we are charging. Hence, some authors propose the hodgepodge accumulation of sigils and their indiscriminate charging. Personally, I give little credit to these practices as superfluous and intellectually somewhat filthy, but the chaoist is free to do whatever he wants.

Spare's favorite method of charging sigils was to achieve emptiness of consciousness through sexuality, specifically autoeroticism. According to Jaq D Hawkins, good old Spare "was known to draw sigils on parchment and seal them

---

55. From Austin Osman Spare's *The Book of Pleasure*, quoted in SEMPLE, G. (1995: 30)
56. MORRISON, G. *Pop magic!*. METZGER, Richard (2014: 20)
57. "Although some would argue that by seeing the sigil every day I'm preventing the manifestation of the desire, I find that after a couple days I have forgotten the purpose of the sigil." ELLWOOD, T. (2008:

into a crucible which was specifically made for sexually discharging himself into, charging the sigil with his own semen. Then, the crucible would be buried and later uncovered for another "charging".[58] Let's not fuss. The frequent use of this very little tantric route for the charging of sigils provides admirable benefits for health: according to the conclusions reached in 2016 by a Harvard T. H.Chan School of Public Health study,[59] based on the monitoring of 31,925 men throughout eighteen years, a monthly ejaculatory frequency greater than twenty reduces the risk of prostate cancer by 20%. Gentlemen are concerned with these conclusions, which settle any possible misgivings regarding the healthiness of the ejaculatory act, but it is undoubted that autoeroticism is at least as beneficial for ladies health, inasmuch as it contributes to the increase in the production of endorphins, dopamine and oxytocin. And also to the reinforcement of self-confidence, an essential factor in the practice of good magic, an issue on which I will expand a little later. Therefore, if some neophyte in search of a method to achieve gnosis is still hesitating between onanism, nausea or self-induced panic, here are some more

---

58 HAWKINS, J. D. (1996: 103)

59 JENNIFER R. RIDER, KATHRYN M. WILSON, JENNIFER A. SINNOTT, RACHEL S. KELLY, LORELEI A. MUCCI AND EDWARD L. GIOVANNUCCI (2016). Ejaculation Frequency and Risk of Prostate Cancer: Updated Results with an Additional Decade of Follow-up. https://www.researchgate.net/publication/299477114_Ejaculation_Frequency_and_Risk_of_Prostate_Cancer_Updated_Results_with_an_Additional_Decade_of_Follow-up

arguments to add to those that you probably already imagined in favor of the first.

Magic, from Tantric to Thelemic, has never underestimated the power of sexuality, and has traditionally drawn on that power for its own purposes.[60]

Has not who reads these lines accused the flaring of their vitality, a greater vigor in their nerves and even the most resolute spirit just by imagining the carnal encounter with the desired person. This sudden invigoration, common among a not inconsiderable percentage of the population, gives us a clue to the driving force of this power. On the other hand, a current as individualistic as chaoism will find no better pretext for the celebration of collective rituals. Chaoism, indeed, but also would-be scoundrels, unfortunately.

Phil Hine warns us of those undesirable agents. Hine, a Chaoist known for his predilection for the collective practice of magic, is, in this sense, a rare author, since chaoists are, as a rule, as has been repeatedly suggested, unlikely to venture outside its individualistic ivory towers. His book *Prime Chaos*, recommended reading for those who wish to enjoy the magic of chaos in company, is an authentic handbook that

---

60. According to the student of Surrealism and Occult Sciences ALEXANDRIAN (2003: 600), «the operations of sexual magic are carried out with seven main objectives: change of fluidic capacitors (that is, of talismans and statuettes to bewitch), production of a magnetic influence that subjects the other member of the couple, realization of a concrete project, determination of the sex of the child to be conceived, refinement of the senses, regeneration of vital energy, trigger of superhuman visions».

documents the details of ritual, so closely related to theater and performance, and breaks down the foreseeable problems derived from the dynamics of a magic group, strikingly similar to those of any other type of collective: cohesion, leadership, organization, conflict, and so on. When the rituals of a group find their way of expression in sexual magic, potential risks arise against which it is better to be on guard. In the first place, those linked to promiscuity, that is, jealousy, spite and all kinds of misunderstandings, even unwanted trade in germs. Hine does not touch on this, but I consider it pertinent to include. Second, and to the dismay of those who profess a virtuous interest in magical practice, the deplorable existence of ignoble individuals, whose feigned affinity for the occult only serves unspoken lubricious aspirations. A devastating vileness, doubly reprehensible as well as vile: because it discredits the honorable tradition of sexual magic. And because pursuing by unnecessarily devious means, what can be honestly achieved with chivalry, a bouquet of flowers and a few gallant words, is nothing but a procedure proper to wretched intellects. Indifferent to technological and social transformation, there are still those who insist on attending demonstrations, choosing a degree or joining secret societies, driven by the same dubious desire. That is why we must be scrupulous and cautious during the selection process for new members. Although even in this way, it is not possible to be completely safe from those who seek to satisfy their base instincts by taking advantage of a group of un-suspecting magicians.⁶¹ Sometimes it is not the novice, but the leader or founder of the group himself who, from the beginning and from a privileged position, has sown the seeds of dishonesty. The list of vicious gurus is endless and pitiful.

And finally there is the danger of laziness: Hine warns, very wisely, that focusing too much on sex causes a decrease in the magical potency of the collective entity. ⁶²

It is appropriate to clarify an aspect regarding the magical force of the group. There is no evidence that this has to be greater than that of a single individual. When Hine, for example, lists the reasons why group magic arouses his sympathy, he cites among others mutual learning, the fun of the matter and the experiential benefit that comes out of the individual shell; but it does not include among them an increase in magic power. Carroll, at first, when he writes *Liber Null & Psychonaut*, is of another opinion: he maintains that, thanks to the synergetic effect, "the collective power will exceed the sum of individual powers participating."⁶³

---

61. See Mircea Eliade's vindications in the mid-1970s, when echoes of psychedelic sex and counterculture still resonated strongly: "The importance of ceremonial nudity and ritual intercourse should not be interpreted as mere products of lusful inclinations. The recent sexual revolution has made these kinds of fictions and prudes obsolete. For the purpose of ritual nudity and orgiastic practices is to recover the sacramental value of sexuality. One could speak of the unconscious nostalgia for a fabulous, paradisiacal existence, free of inhibitions and taboos." ELIADE, M. (1997: 92-93)

62. HINE, P. (2009: 189-190)

63 CARROLL, P. J. (1987: 117)

But barely five years later, in *Liber Kaos*, being congruent with the conclusions that emerge from the famous magic equations that he has elaborated at the time, he affirms that the scores are not cumulative and that "the effects of a number of persons conjuring simultaneously or sequentially for a common objective never exceeds the best result that any one of them might achieve".[64] Despite this apparent contradiction, which in reality is undone in a rectification, and far from being a controversial issue, in the field of chaos magic it seems to be taken for granted that a dozen magicians acting in unison will not achieve what the most seasoned of them cannot achieve alone.

But don't let your spirits drop. It would be a mistake to underestimate the playful component of magic. Hine is not the only one who presents the personal satisfaction emanating from the practice of ritual magic as valuable in itself, regardless of its effectiveness. For Dunn, for example, the fulfillment of a desire is not as important as the stage of euphoria that is reached by practicing magic.[65] The result, the concrete satisfaction of a concrete desire is, in any case, a collateral effect. A lucky side-effect.

This approach, somewhat light-hearted, uncomplexed, and lacking in obsession with results, is mentally healthy, helpful, and typical of chaoism. Its most undesirable counterpart could, of course, be frustration. A magical

---

64. CARROLL, P. J. (1992: 48)

65. DUNN, P. (2005: 8)

activity sustained over time that does not bear fruit is susceptible, especially being in a group, of ending up leading to a demoralizing feeling of wasting time clowning around in partnership. But there is no need to reach that critical point. All authors agree that magic can be fun and effective at the same time. Moreover, it could almost be said that magic has to be both, since it will hardly be effective if it is not fun. Understanding fun in the satisfactory sense, as something worth repeating; not necessarily as something hilarious. Sooner or later, it will cease to be fun if it is not effective. It is about, as in almost everything in this life, finding the right balance point.

Sex, however, is a double-edged sword and has plenty of potential to tip the balance, either spoiling the fun with unnecessary bedding messes or amplifying it to blur the group's founding purpose. In both cases, efficiency suffers. In the first case, the solution will surely go through some divorce, the restructuring of the organizational chart or even, perhaps, the dissolution of the group and a reconsideration of the magic modalities to be exercised in the future. In the second case, by some type of containment that prevents, as Wilhelm Reich would probably add, a waste of valuable orgone energy, that could be used for other purposes. Or, already in a truly grave situation, by seriously considering what is the real purpose of continuing organizing conclaves. Perhaps you have to give up and change the name of the group to another, of the type Society for Encouragement of Joyful Swinging. Which, having reached such a degree of weakening of the initial claims, is not the most tragic end conceivable.

Hine published *Prime Chaos* in 1993, just before the Internet became a mass global phenomenon. His advice, which is still valid, could be summarized as follows: if you want to be part of a magical group and there are none in your area, do not stand idly by, create one yourself. Proactivity above all.

In 1993 that task was more difficult than it is today. It required physical movement, snooping in esoteric bookstores with New Age background music, posting notices on bulletin boards or publishing them in photocopied gazettes, and exchanging private telephones with strangers, among whom some crazy person inevitably sneaked in. But with the Internet and mobile applications there is no excuse, it is enough to look at any social network to immediately find like-minded individuals and conjure, mitigate at least, the danger that a madman who is being harassed in his bedroom by a burning Donald Duck has phoned you at four in the morning.

The search is now too easy and safe. A great majority of authors, whether for ascetic or purely autosuggestive reasons, insist on the convenience that it be the magician himself who (with sweat and boldness, regardless of his manual dexterity or lack thereof) crafts the magical tools that he will use in his ceremonies. According to the same logic and based on the same principle, it must be insisted that you invest your time and effort in the search for confreres. Making the search a real one, a personal immersion in the unknown, not entrusted to cold software designed by third parties, opening loopholes to suggestive contingencies and, why not, to synchronicities. It must necessarily be a source of satisfaction, vital enrichment and magical power that should not be neglected in pursuit of a sterile idleness.

As mentioned before, what is created through ritualism is a space outside the consensual reality, a bubble woven by the intersubjectivity of the participants. The theatrical, the scenographic, plays a fundamental role in this creation of an alternative reality. For this, it is necessary to have a real physical space, conveniently separated from external interference, a room, a rented space, a forest glade in which to build, with the help of a panoply of suggestive tools, decoration, light, sound atmosphere, fragrances and clothing, another space and another time. As proposed, saving distances, forms and objectives. De Sade, Fourier and Loyola in their respective emancipated universes described by Roland Barthes, where their own rules, alien to the profane world, and their own language, alien to the profane ear, must prevail.

This process of reconfiguration requires the involvement of the participants, and this, in the general context of magic, is neither exclusive to chaos magic nor does chaos magic want to be an exception in this. In order to become part of that hiatus in reality, it is imperative before entering, that those involved hang their external roles on the coat rack in the hallway, next to the hat and umbrella. Only then, as one who upon entering a monastic order, leaves his past behind, acquires a new name and puts on a habit, are they in a position to de-personalize and re-personalize themselves. And they cross the threshold of the temple to play a new role, in a kind of rebirth or reincarnation.[66] Hence the adoption of a magical name in the initiation ritual, when the aspirant is accepted into the congregation. Every magician, whether acting in the company of others or alone, whether chaoist or not, bears a magical name. Together with the clothing and the symbols of his own elaboration, by which he defines himself. The magic name makes up his magical personality, his magical Self, his avatar in the multidimensional ether, on the astral plane or whatever we want to call it. I always prefer informational web or field, although I also like the term Mindscape coined by Rudy Rucker, as it is a representation of the qualities to which the magician aspires. What is described here, in short, is the embodiment of a character.[67]

The repeated similarities with the theater should not surprise us, given that the theater itself was born as a mystery-rite, performing a magical function. The theater has long

---

66. "A full length black robe with hood is most excellent for this purpose, as is nudity. A blank, featureless mask completes the effect to total anonymity." CARROLL, P. J. (1987: 117)

67 HINE, P. (2009: 76)

lost that function in the West,[68] but the archetypal and primitive theater, the one that can still be found in the East, whose staging is, according to Antonin Artaud, an instrument of magic and sorcery,[69] remakes, also in his words, "the chain between what is and what is not, between the virtuality of the possible and what already exists in materialized nature."[70]

Magical ritual cannot ignore its intrinsically theatrical nature, just as theater cannot forget its intrinsically magical foundation. In the same way, just as that person from the theater who does not master the magic of the theater is unaware of an essential part of his trade, the magician must train himself in the mastery of the theatrical source, not only scenographic but also dramatic of the ritual, creative imagination, prosody, gestures. The master of ceremonies, a performance that, depending on the group's norms, can be fixed or rotating, is a stage director in the most Artaudian sense of the term. Some openly confront the double discipline by establishing a hybrid and new medium/method,

---

68. «Artaud [...] attempted to revive ritual voodoo theater (banished from Western Culture by Aristotle)—but he carried out the attempt within the very structure (actor/audience) of aristotelian theater; he tried to destroy or mutate it from the inside out. He failed & went insane, setting off a whole series of experiments which culminated in the Living Theater's assault on the actor/audience barrier, a literal assault which tried to force audience members to "participate" in the ritual. These experiments produced some great theater, but all failed in their deepest purpose. None managed to overcome the alienation Nietzsche & Artaud had criticized." BEY, H. (1999: 43)

69. ARTAUD, A. (1999: 84)

70. ARTAUD, A. (1999: 31)

explicitly magical and explicitly theatrical, as is the case of the filmmaker and astrologer Antero Alli and his ParaTheatrical ReSearch, inspired by the techniques of Jerzy Grotowski, Zen Buddhism and Jungian psychology.

As can be seen in the Peter Brook documentary: *The Tightrope*,[71] the ease with which the legendary stage director demonstrates that a few concise instructions are enough for eight actors to synchronize with each other in such a precise way, that it can only be explained as the action of a common mind. That is, the action of a shared thought, which in ethology produces a shoal and in occultism an egregore, partially amends the assertion that group magic does not entail an increase in magical potency.

It may be, as Hine and Carroll have found, that this non-increase is true as far as what the individual magician can accomplish on his own. But taking a look at the list of utilities of the collective ritual proposed by Hine[72], enchantment, meditation, psychodrama, etc., is enough to immediately notice that some of the proposed activities are meaningless or at least limp, if the intention is to address them alone.

Consider, for example, one of the favorite games on the chaoist agenda: the creation of an egregore with the

---

71. BROOK, P. and BROOK, S. (producers) and BROOK, S. (director). (2012). *Peter Brook: The Tightrope*. France: Brook Productions / Cinemaundici. The aforementioned scene, about six minutes long, is found between nineteen and twenty-five minutes, approximately.

72. HINE, P. (2009: 84)

functions of a magical servant. That is, an etheric commissioner of existence, independent of the magician but, at the same time, subject to his Will. It is, to summarize, a spirit, although from a chaoist perspective, that definition can be emptied of any metaphysical component. Resorting to the definition that Dunn attributes to spirits: *collections of symbols with self-awareness*.[73] Well, it is obvious that the collaboration of more than one mind has to contribute in a more viable way to the formation of an egregore, than the simple individual effort.

Allow me to insert at this point a brief parenthesis about the generation of collective minds: the creation of an egregore should never, never be taken lightly. It is an operation that involves serious and very real dangers: carrying it out is much easier than it seems and your product is, in equal measure, easily uncontrollable, so prudence must prevail over the decision to undertake any step in that direction. It is of the utmost importance to resort to it only on specific occasions, to do so only when a specific need requires it, with a very specific and determined purpose. Stick to small groups as much as possible, with the assurance that nothing will escape from conscious control and with the self-imposed mandate to vanquish the egregore once it has fulfilled the agreed objective or, for the sake of even greater caution, when a pre-established term expires that, in no case, should be extended.

---

73. DUNN, P. (2005: 79)

It would seem that I am warning against releasing a beast from the underworld. And in a sense it is. But it is not necessary to resort to magical explanations to argue the reason for my emphatic precautions. Humans exhibit an innate propensity to compose egregores, often unintentionally and even inadvertently. In fact, we do it day after day without noticing the colossal force that unleashes our inattention or, even worse, the vassalage to which such force subjects us. In general, the vassalage is innocuous and does not go beyond the purely playful, but the sympathetic facet has a reverse. It is a phenomenon that Sociologists have studied in detail. A clear illustration of what I am saying can be obtained by taking a look at the various sectarianisms, the ideological mass movements or the stands of a football stadium. It is obvious that none of these cases reflects the mere sum of its individuals, but something else, a common mind, it would be commendable to call it a thought, endowed with a will of its own, sucking up individual minds like a great tentacular psychic leech out from Lovecraft's nightmare. And it makes them parade to the rhythm of his exhalations. Once a certain limit is exceeded, there is a pernicious cumulative tendency that benefits the worst instincts to the detriment of the best, the mess is irreparable and the monster is out of control, in the worst case with catastrophic results. The stinking dump that social media has become is the biggest and most blatant egregore of our time. While appreciating the limited practical benefits that social media have brought, if there were a button that would make them immediately disappear from the face of the Earth, I would not hesitate even half a fraction of a second to press it. But the ball of mental manure kneaded for years with the worst of each of us has grown too large and its deactivation is already as impractical as that of *Skynet* in *Terminator* movies. At this point only an atomic war or a geomagnetic storm and the consequent global blackout could free us from it. Unfortunately, despite the evidence and the repeated lessons of History, collective minds continue to emerge again and again across a wide range of scales, as unstoppable tyrannical monsters only seemingly subjected to the design of who allegedly instrumentalized them. So let us not contribute, out of folly or caprice, to generate more gregariousness, the sonorous kinship between egregore and the gregarious does not cease to amaze me, despite their disparate etymological roots. In short, the conclusion is simple and applicable to any area of life: we do not trigger something that not only will we not be able to control, but will end up controlling us and sucking our brains out.

Fortunately, no one who has been completely dumbfounded would count among his diminished powers the necessary disposition to have reached this paragraph. Whoever has succeeded can resume with me the thread that I left in suspense a few pages ago, when I began to lose myself in ramblings before addressing the convenience of a physical space where to physically celebrate the magical ritual. It should be emphasized that neither the physicality of space nor that of ritual implies a *sine qua non* necessity. It is above all, I reiterate, simply a matter of convenience, since a suitable setting is suggestive and makes things easier. But chaos magic is an intrinsically mental activity. The gestures are symbolic in nature. The magician's wand is not waved to propel the air particles that billow in its vicinity and, depending on some enigmatic domino effect, make them bounce off each other until they form an organized current that pushes the Chinese vase in the hall to levitate above the tablecloth, because that is simply impossible. I'm sorry to disappoint those who place such longings on magic, but the air does not behave like this. The magical gesture, the one that has real effectiveness, is the mental one. That is the one that reverberates in the informational field. Hence, Hine considers *Empty-Handed* magic[74] as perfectly valid and effective, a naked magic that does not use instruments or accessories.

We can say the same about physical space: it is about the physical recreation of our mental symbolic space, even without remaining a mere epiphenomenon. A physical temple is a resonance box, a tool similar to paper whereby the writer pours his inner speech, or the piano that the composer uses to transform the score that he has previously evoked in silence, into sound vibration. In both cases, the creation may have occurred before and its materialization may be due to the needs of communicapability or recording. But what we witness most frequently is a feedback process where the product of the physical act, which is an effect of the exercise of the imagination, in turn nourishes the imagination by becoming its cause, making it difficult to delineate where the abstract conception and its execution

---

74. Hine, P. (2010: 105)

begin, and where they end. And not to mention when we include techniques based on improvisation, automatism and chance in the equation or, going even further, we substitute the pencil or the keyboard for other conscious beings. And in turn endow with will, such as actors and dancers, or even, in some modalities of art or theatrical proposal, the interaction with the audience, in which case we would be again in front of a collective mind.

It is enough, however, that comparison with the arts, not at all trivial, since magic is an art too, to point out that, in the same way that it is the artist's power to choose his tools, it is up to the magician to define the qualities and extent of some tools, according to his claims and personal circumstances.

It is commonplace in most magic books intended for the lay reader to warn of the danger of theoretical laziness, that is understood as over-reading, without practical correlation. Of course, being educated is not only enriching, but also essential. But there is a very human tendency to procrastination, that can lead to indefinitely prolonged passivity. It is paradoxical, because the approach to occult literature is usually carried out with a practical purpose, it is read to know how to do it. At some point, then, you will have to dare to close the book and roll up your sleeves. But the excuses that the neophyte himself concocts to justify the postponement of his royal initiation, whether in a personal capacity or looking for accomplices, trap him in a loop without solution.

Of all the imaginable excuses, two stand out as the most

widespread. The first is to think that you are not yet prepared or that you still do not know enough. It is the perfect way to never be prepared and never know enough, as has been well verified by those who have held the steering wheel of a car in their hands after attending only the theoretical driving classes. The second excuse is the lack of an indispensable infrastructure. Hypothetically indispensable. The list of pre-tasks is so overwhelming! We must start from scratch and, before even pronouncing the first incantation, procure a suitable outfit, empty a room of useless junk, or not, and decorate it properly, assuming we have a room that we can allocate for that purpose, develop magic weapons. Just reviewing the list you get cold sweats. Yes, indeed, being a magician is very difficult.

However, such alibis can be dismantled by confronting them with a basic principle and a suggestion. The basic principle is a classic one and consists, in its canonical meaning, which is what our grandmothers have transmitted to us, that hardly anything worthwhile is achieved without effort; in its restricted sense to magic, it is that the self-discipline required to undertake this effort is, inherently, an essential requirement of the magician. Without self-discipline there is no magic. Therefore, overcoming that initial resistance to getting down to work and the first obstacles, is always easier when we get down to it, by the way, than when we limit ourselves to contemplating them from afar. Henry Ford has already observed that *nothing is especially difficult if we divide it into small tasks*, overcoming that resistance, I say, is not only an unavoidable first step on the path of those who do not wish to remain anchored forever in the calm waters of the armchair of their library. Rather, it is an unavoidable decision of who, indeed, is trained and motivated to overcome other subsequent resistances. It is impossible for someone subjugated by his own evasions to be able to summon the willpower that requires the concentration, perseverance and mental control demanded by magical activity. Control of breathing, emptying the mind with the help, for example, of mantras, focus on one image for hours... Ultimately, it is a circular reasoning that invalidates any exhortation. So do not bother with the laziness in devising subterfuges to excuse one's delay: feel liberated and at peace with oneself, admitting that reading grimoires is enough to meet one's needs.

But there is, as I have already stated, another answer apart from that basic principle, a suggestion that does not deny it, this is indisputable and I will not insist on it anymore. That is more focused on the excuse of the lack of infrastructure, but which is pertinent because the uneasiness caused by this lack can, on occasions, sink its roots more into misunderstanding than in a real need linked to insufficient means. And a misunderstanding can be remedied. Actually, it starts from something that has already been said here: magic is mental and each magician has to determine the elements and characteristics of his own instruments. Therefore, and soon said, this is the suggestion addressed to the neophyte, formulated in the second person singular, *it's up to you.*

This is an unmistakably chaoist invitation. If the aspiring magician has nourished from ancient bibliographic sources, they will have encountered all kinds of detailed instructions and requirements, focused on the celebration of what in that context is understood as an admissible ritual, which can become unnecessarily demoralizing. Fortunately, chaos magic has come to dismantle dogmas, proposing meta-paradigms, non-metaphysical perspectives and free-form rituals, which also encompasses its material scaffolding. Nothing in that scaffolding is mandatory. The magician with desire and resources can complicate themselves as much as they like life, by recreating traditional ceremonies and decorating the cellar of their residence with cauldrons mounted on bronze tripods, covering the walls with gold leaf and composing with marble tessera the mosaic of a pentacle that occupies the entire floor and causes the amazement and admiration of their housekeeper. However, the magic temple can also be small, two-dimensional, deployable, temporary, removable, and even transportable.

A magician who does not have enough space at home, will find inspiration in those films set in the years of Prohibition, in which clandestine gambling dens mock the sudden police interruption by turning the tables. You can take advantage of the available surface on the back of the paintings that adorn your home, move the low table away from the living room to make space and unroll a mat with the magic circle traced with markers, or use removable screens. If you are skilled with DIY, install an endless photostudio bottom tube at the top of each wall to spread wide backdrops that will transform the look of your home with blazing speed and collect them with similar alacrity when it's time for dinner. A large mirror on the bedroom ceiling, in its traditional version or in the cheapest and most affordable version of reflective polystyrene sheet, will allow you to draw, erase and redraw sigils on its surface in order to load them successively with the reflection of the activity officiated between the sheets,[75] which will arouse the healthy envy of your friends and will be a graceful alternative to painting the sigil on the co-participant's face or body, a practice that does not stop being a tacky bit because it enjoys prestige among the chaoists.

And if these ideas still seem complicated or onerous, you can use canvases on a stretcher or a sheaf of colored cardboard and paint on them the symbols of the four elements, as Skinner and King recommend in their manual *Techniques of High Magic*.[76] If you are a friend of miniaturization, you can also put the compressed temple in your desk drawer and, the moment you open it, unfold it as a children's pop-up book. When the temple fits in a briefcase, you can take it on a trip as a ceremonial magic kit and invoke Dormammu from anywhere on Earth, be it a bungalow in Kenya or the narrow bunk of a youth hostel in Santiago de Compostela.

And if you do not want or need a physical temple, or

---

75. It is up to each magician to decide whether the sigil should be traced as is or in a specular arrangement.

76. "They should be painted as brightly as possible; good quality oil paint, enamel paint and poster paint are all excellent for this purpose, but ordinary water-colours should be avoided, they are far too wishywashy." KING, F. and SKINNER, S. (1990: 17)

even having one, you always have the possibility of creating your own astral temple in the astral plane, where you can celebrate your rituals without being forced to resort to a space incardinated in the physical coordinates, as Dunn or Ellwood[77] advise among many others. The use of the term "astral" is customary and does not require further justification, although it is perfectly substitutable for "mental" or "imaginary". Undoubtedly, "astral" has more evocative magical reminiscences, hence its implementation.

The only limits in creating an imaginary temple are those of the imagination, and its construction requires a zero outlay. But that doesn't mean it doesn't require work. Its construction is, in fact, the most arduous. And it is for precisely the same reason that makes it advisable. It requires a great mnemonic effort that the use of tangible objects saves us for obvious reasons: demolitions and gas explosions on the sidelines, the walls of a house will still be there when we return the next day, preserving its width and its layout. Instead, the nature of imaginary structures is liquid and elusive. It tends to fade as the lamp of our consciousness illuminates the successive nooks and crannies. Therefore, you have to work slowly, consolidate what is being developed little by little and, above all, do not pretend to finish the work in one sitting. Not even pretending to finish it. An astral temple is an open work, always capable of being expanded, reformed and perfected.

Outlining the general characteristics of a single stay in

---

77. ELLWOOD, T. (2008: 207-208)

each session is a reasonable goal. This elaboration of a previous scheme, to call it that, will be accompanied in each of its stages by a review of the previous elaborations. The ultimate goal is to achieve, after successive revisions, retouching and additions, a mental image of the astral temple at least as clear and detailed as that of our own home. In other words: the eyes, and other senses, of our imagination have to perceive the representation of the astral temple so clearly, its qualities so concrete and its details so defined as our eyes, and other bodily senses, perceive the appearance, the qualities and the physical details of the house in which our ordinary life runs. And that is not achieved, as some magic manuals usually candidly pretend, conceiving the texture, smell, shapes and definitive traces of the imagined place right away, like someone who obtains something from nothing by snapping their fingers. If anyone doubts that such a prodigy is impractical, they are very free to try it. You will soon discover that a sand castle kneaded in the rain has more overtones of consistency than a barely sketched temple, and that the illusion of sharpness is not sharpness, only illusion. For this reason, despite criteria that I consider wrong in this particular, even if they are more reputable than mine, without any doubt I recommend approaching this task gradually and meticulously, working layer by layer.

Let us therefore undertake, in the same environment and adopting a suitable posture to meditation, the construction of the astral temple starting, from a general decision: What type of temple do we want? Let's try to choose one that is particularly suggestive, both for its aesthetic appeal and for the emotional reverberations it causes in our mood. We all have predilections. Do we prefer a hypogeum, a fortified palace or a primary colors bouncy castle? Are we going for Victorian Gothic or 1970s Brutalist architecture. Would we place the temple high on a summit of perpetual snow, in the clearing of a lush forest, levitating over a sandy desert or in our own city, surrounded by a wall and a decaying garden. That garden, is it Persian, Italian or Zen? If the temple levitates over the desert, do we access it by means of a knotted climbing rope or by a ladder of seventy-two steps. Orientation, height, room number, construction material... Does it have a basement, catacombs that will give us access to buried levels of consciousness, balconies, loopholes, windows. What is the front door like? Is it, in short, a house. It might not be, there are other equally valid alternative spaces to be occupied. For example, a transparent hypercube, formed by the grouping of interconnected cubic rooms. And articulated, so that we can rotate its pieces separately and use it in the manner of Charles Howard Hinton's cubes, as a mental retina to perceive four-dimensional objects. If it's a house, do we make it up entirely, from the foundation to the roof, or are we inspired by something we've seen in illustrations or films? Does it exist or has it really existed? Do we know it well, was our childhood spent in it, is it a place that we once visited and where we have always wanted to return? Options are endless. Once the general is decided, we will undertake the particular. Specific number and relative disposition of rooms, use to which they will be destined, tools and magic furniture that each one of them will contain, accesses, height of the ceilings, type of doors, if any, color of the walls, decoration, flooring, lighting.

The effort maintained, surely throughout several introspection sessions, in this progressive construction, trains the magician's mnemonic and focused imagination capacity. It provides him with a space free from external conditioning, perfectly adjusted to his tastes and needs, at zero cost, available at any time, circumstance and place. Ideal for a wide variety of uses: celebration of rituals, loading of sigils, spiritual retreat, meditation, opening access to the lower floors of consciousness, hyperdimensional contemplation. A communication center embedded in the same web of the informational field, station of departure and arrival of dreamlike incursions. As well as different applications of a more prosaic nature, very profitable for daily life: as a functional artifact at the service of retention, faced with a list that is difficult to remember, one of the most effective mnemonic tricks consists in associating each of its elements with different rooms in a house. As we know well, a remedy against insomnia, promoting narcosis by double bedding: in our bedroom and in the chambers of our astral temple. If we cannot sleep in this way either, at least in the second we will find rest. Or a trick against bad habits, the magician who deprives himself of tobacco with the intention of quitting smoking can, in the worst episodes of crisis, enter a few minutes in the astral temple to smoke a cigarette with the certainty that this punctual non-observance will not damage his lungs.

Even so, especially at the beginning, it is advisable not to trust everything to memory and to force yourself, at the end of each session, to take note of what has been constructed, in the magical diary. An indispensable confidant of any magician, whether chaoist or not. Description can be accompanied by plans or drawings. Even from photographs, why not, if it is an assemblage of pre-existing places. Gathering this information on paper supposes a memory reinforcement and it is advisable to review what has been written down just before undertaking each successive stage. Such annotations are also consistent with the purpose of the magical diary, which is none other, in the first instance, than to serve as a record of magical activity. The construction of a temple is not an activity of another nature, that is why its development must be included together with the rituals performed, the balance of efficiency of the sigils and, even, the review of our dream life if the magician has decided to concentrate everything in a single notebook, there are those who suggest using two for this purpose but it seems unnecessary to me, mainly from the moment in which dream life does not happen beyond our control, that is, from when we have acquired the ability to intervene in it as more than mere spectators.

I am talking about what is commonly known as induced lucid dream, or technique for dreaming while being aware that you are dreaming. It is a method described in 1867 by the pioneer of oneirology, the Frenchman Léon d'Hervey de Saint-Denys in his treatise *Rêves et les moyens de les diriger*, later enriched with contributions from various authors.

Conscious numbness, a necessary procedure to induce lucid dreaming, is greatly facilitated by the availability of an astral temple in which the dreamer can use, taking advantage of the temple's own architecture, a variety of techniques of gradual descent for this purpose. At the same time, it is the induction to lucid dream itself that allows a clear memory of what was dreamed to be maintained when emerging into the waking state, thus enabling its detailed recording in the magical diary.

The lucid experience of dream is in its own right a first order magical experience. It supposes a direct contact with the informational membrane that adds the emitting interaction of the conscious will to the receptor of the common dream, which opens an immeasurable range of possibilities for magical maneuverability, for example vis a vis with other magicians in dream territory. We sleep between 25% and 30% of our lives. Therefore, even if we had no more practical or theoretical contact with magic for the rest of the day, the use of a magical diary and the record of our activity as dreamers would still be fully justified. Paradigmatic are the words with which Howard Phillips Lovecraft begins the story *Beyond the Wall of Sleep*:

> "I have frequently wondered if the majority of mankind ever pause to reflect upon the occasionally titanic significance of dreams, and of the obscure world to which they belong."[78]

---

78. Lovecraft's original manuscript: https://repository.library.brown.edu/studio/item/bdr:734464/

Obviously, with the expression obscure world Lovecraft evokes terrifying insinuations associated with its abyssal cosmogony, populated by ancient mad gods who stalk Humanity from the icy immensity of the Dreamlands. Terrifying warnings for stubborn dreamers like Randolph Carter. But we can also take it in a less threatening sense and understand the obscurity as an allusion to the unknown, to the vast unexplored terrain that only our conscious gaze and interaction will make visible.

Access to the inexhaustible well of experiences and information need not be limited to lucid dreaming. The magician has at their disposal an inverse operation to that of acting in the dream from consciousness, and that is to act in the consensual reality from the dream. That is, to bring out their unconscious in a controlled way during the waking state, the apophenic thinking or the paranoiac-critical method that I will bring up in a moment would result from this operation. This procedure, which can only be assimilated in a trivial way to what is commonly known as daydreaming, is performed with surprising ease when the circumstances are ideal, that is, in hypnagogic periods of semi-unconsciousness, such as those close to waking or light sleep, or also of any other type that facilitates self-immersion in trance.

To mention one of those other examples, I remember the psychedelic experiences that I had as a child when in the Catholic school where I was studying. They made me go to mass so early on Wednesday morning: still fasting, and unable to pay attention to what was happening there, my sight was caught by the candles. Within seconds the physical quality of the space faded and the surrounding gloom became a glowing festival of multi-colored phosphenes that I could manipulate as I pleased. It is unnecessary to emphasize the highly stimulating, lucid and creative condition of such a circumstance. But these are almost accidental cases, subject, as I have already said, to a suitable circumstance. However, the magician can also invoke them at will whatever the circumstance, resorting to a technique that actors, politicians and athletes designate with different names, which in magic is known as glamor and that Neuro-linguistic programming (NLP) defines with a lesser snappy term and much more illustrative: anchor.[79]

It consists of reactivating, through a specific signal, which can be a simple gesture, such as pinching the earlobe, or a verbal password, a psychological state that does not correspond to the current one. This is achieved through a repeated exercise of introspection and evocation of a state that we have already experienced before, that evening in which we conduct ourselves with singular confidence, eloquence or ability to concentrate, but also that meeting in which we were ignored and went unnoticed, in which we anchor the signal that will help us to take possession of that disposition again when it suits us. For example, when we have to face a job interview, an exam or a public appearance, to put only three examples out of the million possible. It is a technique of proven efficacy in the management of one's

---

79. O'CONNOR, J. and SEYMOUR, J. (2008: 92-95)

own emotional states that does not have to be limited to self-confidence or invisibility: it allows, within certain limits, to regulate body temperature or digestive tract processes; and also, of course, in the opposite direction to the activation of lucid dreaming, to dye the waking state with hypnagogic gleams at will. And all this without ingesting entheogens. These dreamless dreams must also be recorded methodically.

I have said before that the claim of the magical diary is to serve as a record in the first instance. This is so because, without detracting from the interest and benefit of mere registration, its ultimate purpose is another, even more important, determining factor in the development and amplification of magical vitality. It is for this purpose and not so much because of notarial zeal that frequent use of the diary becomes imperative. All magicians, from Aleister Crowley to Grant Morrison to Peter J. Carroll, prescribe the daily use, forgive redundancy, of the magical diary. You have to report on it on a daily basis, even if no activity is taking place. The reason is that regular and assiduous journaling increases the chances of success and strengthens self-confidence, which in turn increases the chances of success.

At first glance it is not obvious why such a virtuous circle. The explanation is simple: an insistent examination of the consensual reality, of one's own magical purposes and acts, and of the possible correlation of these with that, together with the conjectures and intertwining of links that inevitably emanate from that examination, inseparable from its daily transcription, educates the mind of the magician in the habit of deliberate practice of apophenic thought, that is, in the adoption of magical consciousness as a map of world events. In this state, the incident that could have gone unnoticed or attributed to causality is immediately justified on a magical basis. If what happens does not happen without reason, but because I have caused it, the confidence in my magical power will be increased and, consequently, also my willingness to persevere. Then my Will will be reinforced and with it my ability to cause changes in reality that, in turn, I will reinterpret.

Apophenia, a tendency to perceive unfounded meaning in random events, and its close relative, pareidolia, a phenomenon in which we mistakenly perceive a recognizable shape in a random image, are creative acts. It is not an adjectival sense, but a substantive one: they are generators of reality. It is surprising that their own definitions contain aporias, such as that, through them we perceive unfounded meanings or that our perception is erroneous. At best, what can be said is that the images or random events have not been deliberately deposited there. But if in the stains of a tile we glimpse a naval battle, that figure exists no less than a naval battle painted in oil on a canvas, because both result from the relationship between stains and colorations. In other words, both images are subjective reconstructions, they are not the naval battle itself, and it is we who have established that relationship, even though the intention and the hand of the artist have previously intervened in the making of the oil.

We project meaning on the reconstruction, and this

meaning can stimulate the understanding of a new reality[80] or a new understanding of reality, of a latent or camouflaged reality. So much so that both apophenia and pareidolia are very useful to archaeologists, for example, in the identification and analysis of prehistoric works. As perceptual and sense-projection tools, they helped us to warn of predators lurking in the foliage and that is why our species has survived, they not only guide us in identifying marks intentionally drawn on the wall of a cave, but also discern why a rock formation with a particular silhouette was worshiped. In the same way, it is from apophenic thought that different procedures of inquiry emanate. Such as the paranoid-critical method that allowed Salvador Dalí to discover the coffin buried in Millet's painting The Angelus, clairvoyance that will later be corroborated by the X-ray analysis carried out in the Louvre Museum laboratories.[81] Or the innumerable systems of divination that the world has known, from oneiromancy, Haruspicy or tarot, to the futurological technique proposed by Alan Moore in his comic *Watchmen*, and practiced by his character Adrian Veidt, consisting of immersing himself in semiotic chaos watching thirty-six television channels at the same time.

---

80. "The occult theory of "signatures" conceives *everything that exists* as a sign and believes its "reading" feasible (the shape of a tree, the location of three or more rocks on a plain, the color of eyes, the marks made by natural forces in an area of natural or artificial terrain, the structure of a landscape, the outline of a constellation, etc.)". CIRLOT, J. E. (1997: 410-411)

81. DALÍ, S. (1998: 16)

It is in this kind of maieutic or socratic method, of shaping some globes of order from the bubbling substance of chaos, and especially in its amplified version, where magic and art come together again beyond the inescapable, and obvious, purely aesthetic or gestural element: as a synthesis of both, according to the express wish of the artist-magician Moore. In a more restricted way, as a hypersigil, according to the term coined by his declared magical arch-enemy, the also comic book writer Grant Morrison, to refer to his work *The Invisibles*.[82]

Art and magic coexist in so many aspects that sometimes it becomes truly difficult to distinguish this from that: expression of the unconscious, plasticity, aesthetics, evocative, cathartic, suggestive and change intention. There is an unequivocally artistic nature in all magic, and there is a manifestly magical art, it was originally cave-dwelling and continues to be so sporadically in ritualistic, mystical or quasi-shamanic performances, even an art with an explicit vocation for transforming society, usually self-described as political art.

However, let us admit that the difficulty in the distinction should not be blamed on magic, whose nature and purpose do not give rise to misunderstanding, but on art, a human manifestation of extremely vague contours. Today, after a long history of transformations and self-questioning in which the twentieth century has played a crucial role, art

---

82. The magical war waged between the two for decades is in the public domain.

has become something tremendously heterogeneous and almost impossible to define. A kind of mixed bag where there is room for an equestrian statue and a court portrait but also a bicycle wheel on a wooden stool, two ditches dug in the desert or a man living with a coyote for three days,[83] that is, almost anything that escapes another cataloging. In this way, works that do not share any common element, neither material, nor intentional, nor contextual, are defined indistinctly as artistic. That is why, depending on the case, of how we limit the artistic phenomenon and what concrete manifestation we use as an example, it can be as true to say that art and magic have nothing in common as, on the contrary, to affirm that they are almost the same.

I say almost because there is an element inherent to magic that, despite its correspondences, will inevitably always keep it at a certain distance from art: it is about its precise and unambiguous intention. An uncertain goal in magic is equivalent to a rubber scalpel in the hand of a surgeon. This is nonsense. On the contrary, ambiguity and polysemy are inherent qualities of art, attributes that, by definition, it cannot do without. Which, by the way, and said without irony, relegates the intention of art to cause change to the realm of desideratum. I think that only the degree of nebulousness of the intention, to call it that, of its level of effectiveness, plain and simple, constitutes a reliable scale to

---

83. With the bicycle, the ditch and the coyote, I am referring respectively to Marcel Duchamp's readymade *Roue de bicyclette* (1913), Michael Heizer's earth sculpture *Double negative* (1969-1970) and Joseph Beuys's performance *I like America and America likes me* (1974).

differentiate certain magical acts from artistic expressions. For the rest, what separates the spheres of art and magic is not a matter for magic and is, in any case, an interesting matter that will be worth analyzing on another occasion and place. I take it for granted that the comparisons I make throughout these pages are based on what unites them, which is a lot. And if an ideogram or a mantra can be a sigil, then a movie, a comic or a symphony can be hypersigil.

Let us look at Morrison's definition: "The hypersigil is a dynamic miniature model of the magician's universe, a hologram, microcosm or 'voodoo doll' which can manipulated in real time to produce changes in the macrocosmic environment of 'real' life".[84] Therefore, hypersigils are conglomerates of sigils arranged according to a pre-established order and whose individual meaning is subject to the meaning of the whole. Exactly the same as the integrating elements of a narrative. Hence, Ellwood defines them as "narrative stories that also function as magical workings by incorporating the magician's desire into the story or other creative process being used."[85]

It should be noted that neither Morrison, nor Ellwood, nor any other chaoist I know of are prolific on this subject. None of them offer details about the hypersigil crafting or charging. Regarding the crafting, perhaps it is fine like that. Vagueness provides fertile ground for speculation and inventiveness. Is hypersigil an explicit display of the sigils

---

84. Grant Morrison, "Pop Magic!". METZGER, Richard (2014: 21)

85. ELLWOOD, T. (2008: 107)

that constitute it, In this case, it should be understood, for example, that the graphic content of each comic strip, or the names of the characters, has been composed according to criteria of sigilization. But perhaps, and this option does not exclude the previous one, hypersigil may also consist of an implicit configuration of individual sigils, for example in their transposition into the narrative structure. In this sense, it occurs to me that the application of the mathematical tools provided by the theory of graphs could be very useful to re-translate, decode and locate the sigils in the underlying framework of the work.

Regarding the hypersigil charge, I personally dare to conjecture two possibilities. The least promising would be a consecutive charge, or serial charge. Something similar to lighting the wick of a string of firecrackers. Out of the Blue it does not seem a way too close to the nature of hypersigil, which by definition does not consist solely of a series of sigils, but of a complex unit of meaning. That is why I lean more towards the second possibility: that of a hypercharge.

This is something to which we are not strangers who in secular reality, have been involved in the realization of works destined for public exhibition, such as a comic, in Morrison's case. Or a film, a book, a theatrical play or a musical composition and I stop here out of restraint, but nothing really prevents us from lengthening the list to less artistic products, such as a new model of toothbrush or an operating system. The hidden goal to which we have all aspired, and I say hidden because that goal is not always explicitly contemplated, not even consciously, is to delegate the charge of the work or the hypersigil to the audience. In other words, the purpose, both in the dissemination of an artistic work and in that of a hypersigil, is its viralization, the creation of an egregore. That hackneyed phrase that once the work reaches the hands of the public it becomes independent from its author and embarks on its own vital journey, acquires all its meaning here. Hypersigil would thus be, from this conception, a complex artifact programmed to be activated by collective thought and destined for a univocal purpose, predetermined by the magician.

We are nearing the end and it is time to ask ourselves if magic, once emptied, or, rather, exempted, of metaphysical premises, is nothing more than a game of the mind focused exclusively on personal transformation and the stimulation of the creativity. That is, if sticking to the essentials, there is a real difference between sending sigils and painting watercolors on Sundays. Once the preternatural entities and energies not recognized by science have been discarded, or, rather, relegated, it is legitimate to ask what net contribution does the magic of chaos, postmodern make? Or the heterodox magic of the 21st century, in addition to present an eclectic conglomeration of ideas and procedures already contributed by other disciplines, a cocktail with some NLP, theater, Jung, conceptual art, grandma's remedies, lucid dreams and a hodgepodge of speculations on chaos theory and contemporary cosmology not exempt from dilettantism? Isn't it, since it's more magic for skeptics, less magic? Isn't it something difficult to define, perhaps comforting, perhaps even suggestive to some people, but ultimately something decidedly not magical? They are reasonable doubts that deserve an answer. Next I am going to try to synthesize what we could call a colophon.

As much as the style, the means and the pretexts have changed, the neuralgic foundation of magic, which consists in the intention of causing changes in reality in accordance with our Will, has not changed one iota since our most remote ancestors articulated their first spells. To which we should add that if magic has been reduced to a cocktail of NLP, art, dreams, chaos and so on, it is equally reasonable to rotate the binomial and proclaim that the aforementioned cocktail of ingredients constitutes in itself, for all intents and purposes, the genuine stuff of magic. And if the result of the intrinsic intention to change reality did not offer, going to the extreme, more but also no less than personal transformation and the stimulation of creativity, would there be cause for complaint. Or is it all about minutiae?

Ultimately it would be a problem of interpretation. Because, although the profane observer could understand it that way, it could not be from a magical mentality, according to which the inner change is never detached from the outside. Either by reciprocal influence, as both are changes in the same substance, according to some authors, or because the so-called objective reality is subsumed in the subjective one. Since we live life subjectively, what happens objectively, outside our sphere of perception, has little relevance. After all, a certain degree of solipsism, however attenuated it may be, is inseparable from magical thinking. Even in ordinary experience: does it really matter whether the tree makes a noise when it falls or not, when no one else can hear it? And yet the recourse to the last resort is unnecessary, since the change in objective reality is real, not an interpretation of the facts, as I am going to now explain.

There is a story that I like to tell. It hardly exceeds the condition of an anecdote, but within its modesty it marks a difference with respect to other unusual events that I have related previously. On a certain occasion, just at the beginning of this century, and due to my cinematographic work, I had the need to establish contact with a specific person. I did not have her phone number and, in those circumstances, the only way to access it would have been to show up at her place of work. Something that did not involve any difficulty except the movement itself, a route that, without being long, required a time that I did not have. In the days that followed, while I was delaying the decision to physically go to meet her, something puzzling happened on the street. On three consecutive occasions, at the rate of one a day, I stumbled upon one, two, and even three people whom I had not seen for many years and whom I had not heard from in all that time, but in who, curiously, had thought the night before.

Note that I am talking about highly unlikely confluences in a city inhabited by several million people; and not from a single chance encounter, but from three in a row. Such recidivism made such an impression on me that I resolved to completely stop worrying about getting the phone number or looking for gaps in my schedule to go to the work of the person I wanted to approach. I just waited with the firm certainty that shortly, that same week, I was going to run into her. I did it with absolute conviction, but without encouraging any kind of effort to concentrate or intensify the desire, relegating it to the unconscious. I simply busied myself with other matters, assuming the meeting was going to take place. So it was. The meeting took place without an appointment the next morning, with unmistakable punctuality, on a busy subway platform where we had never met before.

I do not want to reiterate with this memory what I have already stated regarding the unscientific, or directly unscientific, condition of figuratively rationalist assertions that seek to confine an event of these characteristics in the trunk of chance. How many probabilities does a chance-based explanation give the unbroken fourfold coincidence of previously foreshadowed encounters in an urban context? One in trillions. In my opinion, such an unmotivated denial, bordering on the foolish, can only emanate from prejudice. It is not worth dwelling on. As soon as each one of us begins to recapitulate, it is evident that there must be a non-random *why* behind the quadruple coincidence, and the vision of Achacachi, and the limousine stopped in front of the cemetery and of so many and so many other oddities that occur much more frequently than is conventionally assumed. But this has already been said.

Where I want to go with my account of the encounters is one step further, because what differentiates this case from the others, from those I have told and from others I have not told, is that in this case, for the first time, I was not content with playing the role of mere spectator. I think I can firmly affirm that having experienced the first three encounters in a more or less passive way, not premeditated in any case, was what prompted me to provoke the fourth. It is in the intentionality of this act, in the determination to generate a voluntary change in reality, assisted by an unknowable causal mechanism, that its genuinely magical nature lies.

It may be objected that the fourth encounter could have happened anyway and that, consequently, the influence of the will on reality is not necessarily irrefutable. Such an objection strikes me as childish. Considering the infinite multiplicity of derivatives that can arise from a minimal alteration of behavior, it is evident that denying magical interference returns us to the spiral of denials linked to computations based on a chance so inconceivable, that it could be said to be endowed with the malice of a gambler. The simple fact of brooding over the three preliminary meetings and choosing to trust the advent of a fourth instead of, for example, checking that my calendar did not actually collect the phone number of some common acquaintance who could act as an intermediary. It would have been enough to arrive three seconds late at the pedestrian crossing and be impelled by the red traffic light to take any detour, as I continued walking down the street, instead of going down to the platform, frustrating the encounter.

But the case in question is important for one more reason. The decision to wait for the encounter, that is, to provoke it, succeeds another of greater scope. The decision to give credibility to the chain of synchronicities, to apply an apophenic interpretation to that chain and to act in accordance with a magical principle. In other words: the magical act obeys a voluntary change of mentality. A deliberate, rational change, the result of a choice. Because, just as magical thinking is a way of reasoning rooted to a greater or lesser degree in the unconscious of any healthy individual, it is convenient, for the sake of sanity, to keep it at bay. And, to not recklessly disrupt the logical connections that guarantee a sensible discernment, subject to the verdict of the facts. To use magical thinking when, where and in the way, in which it can be useful to us, is a discretionary decision.

That decision is a trigger that, if it persists over time, becomes a way of life. Encouraged by some type of small but resounding success such as the one reported, it is understandable that the decision maker will decide again and again, when he witnesses a significant coincidence, feeding back his conviction in the value of his insistence and increasing his level of alertness before new possible matches. Adopting, finally, Apophenia as a system of apprehension and habitual resolution.

Having originated this perceptual and behavioral change in a punctual volitional act, and glimpsing it with the power of performative statements, the word of Alan Moore, alluded to at the beginning of this essay, should no longer surprise us. He maintains that it is enough to declare oneself a magician to be one. Even if it's for a day. Then you have to exercise. But it will hardly be stopped when chaos has made sense and magic has become ubiquitous and is at hand. Up to that point the change of perception is decisive. The opening of the mind to unsuspected connections. And it will not be just, as I have already anticipated, a subjective transformation. Not anymore, from then on.

It is well known that transmuting lead into gold was for the ancient alchemists nothing more than, at best, an inconsequential result of their inner transmutation; the one they really sought. Or, more commonly, a subterfuge, a strategy to cover up their true purposes and avoid the suspicion of the guardians of the faith, who at that time did not show great compromise with heretics. Who, in a flash, sent them to atone for their sins at the stake.[86] It is also known, and it has been said here, that magicians of all ages have led themselves with an equivalent pretense. And that in no way do the chaoists represent a schism in that tradition. As Hawkings is apt to point out, by resorting to the parallelism between chaoists and alchemists.[87]

---

86. To the false alchemists, that is, to those who only aspired to external transmutation, that of metals, and also to those swindlers who, while being aware of their lack of skill in bringing the aforementioned prodigy to fruition, took advantage of the ingenuity of any prince or potentate willing to defray the expenses of a laboratory and a comfortable life, that is, to all those who considered themselves alchemists without being alchemists ?and the fundamental difference was based on their motivations?, the title of *blowers* was reserved for them. The meaning of such qualification is derived from the action of fanning the flames of the atanor with a bellows in an unsuccessful way.

Still, it would be a mistake to interpret the change in objective reality as a metaphor for subjective change. A transformation of mentality, which implies a sustained reordering of thoughts over time, implies a real, measurable physical change. Rearrangement is mental and also material. The brain readjusts and reconfigures itself. Not only at the software level, but physically: it readjusts its hardware by reconfiguring the neural links, making some disappear and weaving new networks that come to replace the previous ones. We constantly mold our brain mass without noticing it and, of course, so does the magician. Although the magician must be aware.

We have not yet left the interior of the skull and a direct interaction between mind and matter has already become evident. It is an byproduct of the interest in magic and its implementation. How can we not admit, then, without ambiguity, the multifaceted range of modifications in external reality that magic has the potential to generate. Unless we are in complete solitude floating in the middle of the Atlantic, if that reality is above all, more than a material one, more than a conglomeration of waves and particles, a symbolic universe. A network of inter-subjectivities, that is, a consensual reality, a construction of and with others. In what way could the effective interaction with this consensual reality be illusory for those who, from their behavioral procedure, expressly perceive, pulse, tense and tear the

---

87. "A Chaos Magician understands that whatever methods are used are no more than an outward dosplay of an inner transformation. The alchemists of the past pursued inner transformation, yet wrote of the transmutation of metals." HAWKINS, J. D. (1996: 81)

sensitive membrane that constitutes that reality?

Let's take the opportunity to redefine the illusory. Because anyone endowed with the ability to move one meter forward is in a position to move the entire cosmos one meter in the opposite direction. Walking three steps in the direction of the Pole Star, is the exact equivalent of standing still and drawing the Pole Star, three steps in our direction. Every time we jump, we return to the ground with the same force with which the Earth returns to our feet, because the gravitational attraction is mutual. These commensurable interactions with the great material universe will be minuscule, perhaps childish, and surely even irrelevant for practical purposes, but by no means illusory. Let's hold back the laughter the next time someone claims that they can move a galaxy with their finger, lest they actually can.

Adopt a point of view that helps to question the prefabricated illusions and opens the mind to possibilities. That moment, such as extracting an inexhaustible flow of riches from the well of the unconscious, amplifying the intuition. Tuning. what in other times was called the sixth sense. Intervening creatively in chaos, especially as assures Grant Morrison, when the effectiveness of sigils is absolute. Reinforcing our ability to control the rudder of our existence, with power and responsibility, must necessarily be rewarded with invaluable intimate satisfaction. It endows the existence of a complementary meaning in some cases, and even a full meaning in others. Definitely, since the birth of chaoism, which does not even have to conflict with empirical science, since they are systems of thought sometimes confluent, sometimes parallel, that run along independent routes.

In the end, and to conclude, one thing must be taken into account: each and every one of us, to a greater or lesser extent throughout our lives, exercises creativity. We perceive pareidolias, we tune in with flashes of clairvoyance, we contribute to the formation of egregores, we let ourselves be carried away by intuition in making decisions, we are anchored to behaviors, habits, addictions and psychic states that we do not govern. We adopt different roles, personality masks, depending on who we have in front of us. We participate in the dream life. We are hostages of the passions and erotic drives. We need to develop profitably in the social fabric. We feel the power of performative statements and we are, in short, assiduous recipients of the magic wielded by third parties. It is an inevitable phenomenological context, inherent to human existence. In front of it there are several positions. Regardless of nominalist labels and debates, you can turn your back on it and deny the evidence, accept it without taking sides or decide to take the path of the magician: take an active, conscious and voluntary role in that context.

The kind of magic most in keeping with the times and freest from monomania, stagnant structures, and the scent of mothballs, is chaos magic. Its practice is an exercise of freedom, but in a broad sense: not only because of what it means to choose, but because of the continuous demand for freedom that its implementation requires. The risks of this practice, generally identical to those that we would find in other forms of magic, have been explained. Its effectiveness can be debated, as can its theoretical foundations. As much as there are personal benefits and satisfaction, the frustration it can bring is something that belongs to the subjective realm. And it may not help make the world a better place, but, it makes it more interesting.

Carlos Atanes
Madrid, May 2018

BIBLIOGRAPHY

ALEXANDRIAN. Historia de la filosofía oculta. Francisco Torres Oliver (trad.). Madrid: Valdemar [Enokia S.L.], 2003. ISBN: 84-7702-432-4

ARTAUD, Antonin. El teatro y su doble (1ª ed., 9ª reprint). Enrique Alonso and Francisco Abelenda (trad.). Barcelona: Edhasa, 1999. ISBN: 84-350-1502-5

BEY, Hakim. Inmediatismo. Carlos Barona (trad.). Barcelona: Virus Editorial, 1999. ISBN: 84-88455-56-9

CARNEGIE, Dale. Cómo ganar amigos e influir sobre las personas (16ª ed.). Román A. Jiménez (trad.). Barcelona: Edhasa, 2018. ISBN: 978-84-936649-2-3

CARROLL, Peter J. Liber Kaos. York Beach (ME): Samuel Weiser, Inc., 1992. ISBN: 0-87728-742-2

CARROLL, Peter J. Liber Null & Psychonaut. San Francisco (CA): Red Wheel/Weiser, LLC, 1987. ISBN: 978-0-87728-639-4

CIRLOT, Juan Eduardo. Diccionario de símbolos. Madrid: Ediciones Siruela, 1997. ISBN: 84-7844-798-9

CROWLEY, Aleister. 777 Revised. Ulthar - Sarkomand - Inquanok - Leeds: Celephaïs Press, 2004.

CROWLEY, Aleister. Magick in Theory and Practice. York Beach, Maine: Samuel Weiser, 1994. ISBN: 9780877287377

CULIANU, Ioan P. Eros y magia en el Renacimiento. Neus Clavera and Hélène Rufat (trad.). Madrid: Ediciones Siruela, 1999. ISBN: 84-7844-441-6

DALÍ, Salvador. El mito trágico de "El Ángelus"de Millet. Joan

Vinyoli (trad.). Barcelona: Tusquets Editores, S.A., 1998. ISBN: 84-8410-585-3

DUNN, Patrick. Postmodern Magic: The Art of Magic in the Information Age. St. Paul, MN: Llewellyn Publications, 2005. ISBN: 0-7387-0663-9

ELIADE, Mircea. Ocultismo, brujería y modas culturales. Enrique Butelman (trad.). Barcelona: Ediciones Paidós Ibérica, S.A., 1997. ISBN: 84-493-0400-8

ELLWOOD, Taylor. Multi-Media Magic: Further Explorations of Identity and Pop Culture in Magical Practice. Stafford, UK: Immanion Press - Megalithica Books, 2008. ISBN: 978-1-9057113-14-1

FARBER, Philip H. Meta-magick : the book of atem : achieving new states of consciousness through NLP, neuroscience, and ritual. San Francisco (CA): Red Wheel/Weiser, LLC, 2008. ISBN: 978-1-57863-424-8

FREUD, Sigmund. El malestar en la cultura. Ramón Rey Ardid (trad.). Madrid: Alianza Editorial, S.A., 1997. ISBN: 84-206-6363-8

GUÉNON, René. Símbolos fundamentales de la ciencia sagrada. José Luis Tejada and Jeremías Lera (trad.). Barcelona: Ediciones Paidós Ibérica, S.A., 1995. ISBN: 84-493-0136-X

HAWKINS, Jaq D. Understanding Chaos Magic. Chieveley (Berkshire), UK: Capall Bann Publishing, 1996. ISBN: 1-898307-93-8

HINE, Phil. Condensed Chaos. An introduction to Chaos Magic (2ª ed. / 9ª reprint.). EE.UU.: Falcon Press, 2010. ISBN: 978-1-935150-66-4

HINE, Phil. Prime Chaos. Adventures in Chaos Magic (3ª ed. revised). EE.UU.: Falcon Press, 2009. ISBN: 978-1-935150-67-1

HINTON, Charles H., STOTT, Alicia Boole, FALK, H. John. A

New Era of Thought. EE.UU.: Andesite Press, 2015. ISBN: 1297501071

KING, Francis and SKINNER, Stephen. Técnicas de Alta Magia. Juan José Alonso Rey (trad.). Madrid: Luis Cárcamo, editor, 1990. ISBN: 84-7627-057-7

KUHN, Thomas S. La estructura de las revoluciones científicas (3ª ed.). Carlos Solís Santos (trad.). México, D.F.: Fondo de Cultura Económica, 2006. ISBN: 968-16-7599-1

LÉVI, Eliphas. Dogma y ritual de la alta magia (11ª ed.). Buenos Aires: Editorial Kier, S.A., 1992. ISBN: 950-17-0903-5

METZGER, Richard (Ed.). Book of Lies. San Francisco (CA): Red Wheel/Weiser, LLC, 2014. ISBN: 978-1-938875-10-6

O'CONNOR, Joseph and SEYMOUR, John. Introducción a la PNL. Barcelona: Ediciones Urano, S.A.U., 2008. ISBN: 978-84-7953-096-9

PEAT, F. David. Sincronicidad (3ª ed.). Darryl Clark y Mireia Jardí (trad.). Barcelona: Editorial Kairós, S.A. 1988. ISBN: 84-7245-295-6

RASULA, Jed y MCCAFFERY, Steve (Ed.). Imagining language: an anthology. Cambridge (MA): The MIT Press, 1998. ISBN: 0-262-18186-X

SEMPLE, Gavin W. Zos-Kia An Introductory Essay on the Art and Sorcery of Austin Osman Spare. London: BCM Fulgur, 1995. ISBN: 978-1558183421

STEINER, Rudolf. La cuarta dimensión. Geometría sagrada, Alquimia y Matemática. Buenos Aires: Editorial Antroposófica, 2016. ISBN: 978-987-682-1414

If you enjoyed this book
and want to know more
sign up for free Mandrake monthly book newsletter, here's how:
Visit the
mandrake.uk.net
website
A subscription page should pop-up

or type this link into a browser

http://eepurl.com/THE9P